JERSEY 14p

2nd

1st

*Christmas
stamps*

60

Wildlife Conservation
Christmas 1980

ISLE OF MAN 8p

30

Christmas
1982

11p

ISLE OF MAN

WADDINGTON 1982

41

ROAD

65

E

45

Beatrix Potter included a robin in five paintings out of 26, in
The Tale of Peter Rabbit, first published in 1902 (Frederick Warne & Co.),
but she never mentioned them in her text

'Robin'
by Sophie-May Lewis

REDBREAST

The Robin in Life and Literature

by

ANDREW LACK

.....

based on the book
ROBIN REDBREAST
by
David Lack

.....

Foreword by Richard Mabey

.....

Illustrated in colour and black and white
Cartoon illustrations by Euan Dunn

SMH

British Library Cataloguing in Publication Data

A catalogue record for this book is available from
the British Library.

ISBN 978-0-9553827-2-7

© Andrew Lack

First published 2008 by
SMH BOOKS
Pear Tree Cottage, Watersfield, Pulborough
West Sussex, RH20 1NG
www.smh-books.co.uk

Typeset by
MusicPrint, Chichester

Printed and bound in Great Britain by
Ashford Press, Gosport, Hampshire

REDBREAST

The Robin in Life and Literature

by

Andrew Lack

'An intimacy with a robin ... is a liberal education.'

Frances Hodgson Burnett

CONTENTS

ACKNOWLEDGEMENTS

We acknowledge with thanks the granting of permissions for copyright material to be reproduced in this book, by the following publishers, agents and persons:

John Murray (for an extract from THE HON. SEC., by John Betjeman); by kind permission of Kieron Griffin, as Trustee for the Mrs H M Davies Will Trust Davies (two extracts from MY BIRDS, and ROBIN REDBREAST, IN THE SNOW, THE TRUTH, and PEACE AND GOODWILL by W H Davies); Mrs Ruth Lowbury and Carcanet (for SNOW and LATE AUTUMN from *Selected Poems* by Andrew Young); Carcanet (for THE CHRISTMAS ROBIN from *Complete Poems in One Volume* by Robert Graves); Sue Cowling (for her REQUIEM FOR A ROBIN from *What is a Kumquat?,* Faber & Faber, 1991); David Higham Associates (for DECEMBER SONG and A TURN FOR THE BETTER from *Collected Poems* by Norman Nicholson, and for an extract from *The New Book of Days* by Eleanor Farjeon); The Literary Trustees of Walter de la Mare and the Society of Authors as their representative (for an extract from THE FEATHER, and A ROBIN, and two poems, entitled WINTER, by Walter de la Mare); The Society of Authors as the Literary Representative of the Estate of Rose Fyleman (for THE ROBIN by Rose Fyleman); Mrs Rosemary Vellender, Executor of the Estate of Edward Thomas (for an extract from DIGGING by Edward Thomas); David Higham Associates (for FEBRUARY by Francis Brett Young); Pollinger, Proprietor of the Estate of Richard Church (for ANY SMALL ROBIN and an extract from *The Voyage Home* by Richard Church); Faber & Faber (for ROBIN SONG from *Crow* and ROBIN from *The Iron Wolf* by Ted Hughes); Lucas Alexander Whitley (LAW) (for ROBIN from *Snow Water* by Michael Longley); Michael Levy (for his MOTHERS NEVER DIE, written for International Women's Day, 2004); Random House (for an extract from *Watchers of the Wild*, Hutchinson, 1945, and for THE REDBREAST from *The Inn of Birds* by Anthony Rye, Jonathan Cape, 1947, James Kirkup (for his THE REDBREAST, INSPIRED BY AN ENGRAVING BY THOMAS BEWICK);

Polygon, an imprint of Birlinn Ltd (for BIRDS ALL SINGING from *Riding Lights*, 1955; and REAL LIFE CHRISTMAS CARD, by Norman MacCaig); Bloodaxe Books (for an extract from CAROL OF THE BIRDS by Anne Stevenson, from *Poems, 1995-2005*, by kind permission of the author and publisher); Mrs Robin Ravilious (for extracts from A SEDATIVE AT DAYBREAK from *The View from this Window*, 1946, and FLIGHT, from *In time of Suspense*, 1940); Kit Wright (for his THE SUB-SONG); Sandra MacGregor Hastie (for ENCOUNTER WITH AN OLD ROBIN).

Frederick Warne & Co. (for an illustration from *The Tale of Peter Rabbit* by Beatrix Potter, (© Frederick Warne, 1902, 2002); Leeds Museum and Galleries (City Art Gallery), UK/the Bridgeman Art Library (for 'Robin', from *The Farnley Book of Birds,* c.1816, a pencil and watercolour on paper by J M W Turner); Alexander Library, Oxford University Libraries Service (for the photograph of Viscount Edward Grey); Sophie-May Lewis, for her photograph: 'Robin'.

Every effort has been made to contact copyright-holders so that permissions might be granted and due acknowledgements, made. Where, inadvertently, we have failed in this endeavour, we apologise and invite any concerned to contact us, if they so wish.

FOREWORD

After a poll in the *Times* in 1960, the robin was elected to the status of Britain's national bird. There scarcely seems to have been a time when it wasn't. As Andrew Lack's rich reworking of his father's anthology *Robin Redbreast* shows, the bird has always been there in a corner of our hearts. A 12th century document from the Abbey of Furness describes how a much-loved tame robin was restored to life by St Kentigern. Eight hundred years later, Kit Wright's poem 'The Sub-song' suggests another kind of revival, the wistfulness of all singletons given meaning by the robin's winter murmurings: "I can sing, I am here, I exist, perpetually."

In between, almost every poet – Chaucer, Wordsworth, Ted Hughes – has lauded the bird for its boldness, its brightness, its beneficence. There are no truly great robin poems, like Hughes' 'Swifts' or George Meredith's 'The Lark Ascending'; the robin simply isn't that kind of heroic, elusive creature. Its literature has a clarity and directness that echo those of the bird itself. There's little of the mysterious ambivalence with which we've always wreathed that darkling bird, the nightingale; or the symbolic insubstantiality into which skylarks disappear as they climb into 'the steepy air'. Robins are unambiguous, democratic, up-front.

What's fascinating is the near unanimity in a thousand years of writing about the qualities that give the bird its appeal. Some are the homely virtues, the confidingness that can bring robins' domestic lives so close to ours. Their willingness to nest almost anywhere, for instance, famously in an unmade bed, a gardener's jacket pocket (built between breakfast and lunch), the skull of a man hanged for highway robbery in 1796. Their enjoyment of human company (there are many stories of robins which live in churches, and join in the singing). Their loyalty, their lack of pretence, their bad-weather sturdiness. There is a hint of moral approval in our love of the birds, even a sense that we glimpse our own imagined national characteristics in their behaviour: the robin - named probably from Robin Goodfellow – as an avian John Bull, a flighted oak. And our fond notion that only British robins will perch on garden forks does indeed have a mite of scientific truth behind it.

 For myself, I think the robin's eyes have a lot to do with it, those pert, piercing beads, 'like black dewdrops', as Frances Hodgson Burnett describes them in *The Secret Garden*. (The robin, of course, plays a key role in the story, showing Mary where the key to the garden is hidden, and then leading her to the door.) Robin's eyes are side-mounted, like most birds'; but in that classic robinesque cock of the head, they seem to look directly at us. We're caught in the frankness of that gaze, confronted by an unafraid, unthreatening being as we rarely are by any other creature. No wonder we melt, and feel for a moment that we both live in the same one world.

© Richard Mabey

INTRODUCTION

This book is a new edition of ROBIN REDBREAST written by my father, David Lack, published in 1950 and long out of print. I have modified, updated and extended the book but hope that I have retained the spirit of the original. I have drawn from many further publications, especially those that have appeared since 1950 and others that my father may have missed, or omitted.

There can be few birds that evoke such affection in Britain as the robin and REDBREAST is a tribute to the bird that, more than any other, has become part of British life. So much so that, in 1960, after a lengthy correspondence and poll in *The Times* newspaper, it was declared our national bird. The popularity is based on several things. First, it is one of our commonest birds and strongly associated with human habitation. The British Trust for Ornithology estimates that there are between five and six million robins in the UK, the number remaining fairly stable. Secondly, it is tame in Britain, is a frequent companion to gardeners and can readily be trained to take food from the hand. Thirdly, it is not only attractive to look at, but its liquid warbling song can be heard at almost all times of year. It is particularly valued in the autumn when almost no other birds are singing.

The robin has inspired a great quantity and variety of literature over the centuries. Pastoral poetry is the best-known but it has featured in a remarkable number of other ways: in Elizabethan murders, in eighteenth century politics and in the Victorian nursery; it has attended a queen's funeral in Westminster Abbey and the execution of a pauper outside a county jail; it has been lectured on by Ruskin in Oxford; restored to life by a Saint in Fife and even poisoned at the Crystal Palace! Its association with Christmas, especially with Christmas cards, is an essential part of British life. Numerous natural history books discuss its habits and in the last hundred years much scientific study has been done. It was one of the first birds to receive its own biography, *The Life of the Robin* by David Lack (1943).

The selection is, naturally, a personal one, from the great range on offer. I have tried to include not only the best robin poems but also the whole range of ways in which it has been included in literature. There were sufficient robin poems to inspire two anthologies in the early nineteenth century: *Tales of the Robin, and other Small Birds,* by Joseph Taylor in 1815, containing 25 robin poems, and *The Robin's Jubilee,* published by T.Gosden, London in 1826, with 63 poems (including a few of Taylor's). Many more poems and anthologies have been written since. Much of the verse, especially of the late eighteenth and nineteenth centuries, is sentimental or trite, or both. I have only included a little of this, to give a flavour. There have been many prose writings about the robin, particularly children's stories. I have included extracts from the most significant of these and some especially striking passages or references where robins play a prominent role. I have omitted nearly all passing literary references to robins, usually when it is mentioned as one of several possible birds. The majority of the numerous natural history books that mention the robin, some quite extensively, and the scientific study of robins, dating mainly since 1950, are not included.

I have included some Irish writers. Irish literature falls within the same tradition and they have a similar relationship with the robin. A few digressions occur into robin literature from outside these islands, when they illustrate something not present in the British literature.

I have used standard editions for the references included here. For the poetry written before about 1600, the original words and spelling are retained, with footnotes where needed. For some of the extracts written after this, a little updating of the spelling has been included. The one exception is John Clare, represented by more extracts than any other writer. Clare used almost no punctuation and occasional idiosyncratic spelling. Only some of his work was published during his lifetime. Punctuation has sometimes been added in subsequent editions, both of previously published and unpublished work, although most recent editions leave it as he wrote it. This gives rise to some ambiguities in meaning but can increase the appreciation of the poems, so here I have left Clare's poems without additional editing.

The name

The name 'Robin' is a friendly nickname. In Anglo-Saxon, the bird was a 'Ruddock', and the early English name was 'Redbreast'. Other European names reflect its red breast, such as Rougegorge, Pettirosso, and Rudzik. There is also our favourite outlaw, Robin Hood, and the friendly sprite, Robin Goodfellow. The derivations of these are likely to be different. For the bird, it may simply be an alliterative nickname or derived from the Latin *rubens* (red), or possibly the Frisian 'robijnste', meaning a linnet - another red bird, or the Dutch 'robijn', meaning a ruby. Robin Hood is more likely to derive from the Norse or perhaps French for a she-devil or ram, Goodfellow being a euphemism for the same person[1]. Despite this, they have become the same and the persistence of a nickname, rather than its creation, implies personal friendship and is how it has been understood for many centuries.

Not many other birds have nicknames. There is Jenny Wren, in folklore regarded as the mate, or the enemy, of the Robin, Jack-daw, Mag-pie and occasional others. It has been called simply 'robin' since 1549 at the latest, and the name was given official status by the British Ornithologists Union in 1952, though the name redbreast does reappear, as in Wordsworth's poetry. The robin may occasionally have had other nicknames but nearly all are variants of Robin or Bobby[2], and there is no definite evidence of a persistent nickname outside Britain. The reason seems clear: it is only in Britain that it is tame almost everywhere. Further north, the winters are too severe for the bird to stay. In fact, some migrate to Britain from Scandinavia. In southern Europe, they have had good reason to avoid mankind. While the British have been feeding robins, robins have been feeding the French, Italians, and others! European Union legislation from 1979 has made trapping of them illegal, but this is regularly flouted.

---

1   The French word *robinet*, meaning a tap, comes from the fact that they were shaped like ram's heads on rustic fountains. See Robert Graves *The White Goddess* for much further discussion on both the etymology and its implications.

2   Wordsworth mentions 'Peter of Norway and Thomas of Finland' (Chapter 8) and Bewick and, recently, Francesca Greenoak in *All the Birds of the Air* (1979), Thomas Gierdet and Tommy-liden but these are, at most, local and have not persisted.

Anyway, it will take many more decades and a widespread change of attitude to allow the robin to become as tame as it is in Britain. The robin's place around the homestead, and in English literature, is due to the combination of mild winters and kindness towards birds.

The popularity of the British robin has meant that other birds have been named after it, usually because of a red breast – for instance, in North America (a thrush), in Australia (a group of flycatchers), and elsewhere. The most well-known of these is the American robin, a migratory thrush common through much of North America, which has inspired its own literature, not included here. The name has also given an association with the bird to certain people named Robert, groups with red uniforms, and some other red or domestic objects. Many of these have been written about with the bird in mind, or have incorporated the bird into an emblem (Chapters 6 and 7). Curiously, the male of the hobby, but not the female, has also been known occasionally to falconers as a 'robin'. This has caused a little confusion (Chapter 7).

'Robin' is used for at least nineteen different British plants, according to Geoffrey Grigson, in *The Englishman's Flora*. It is the standard vernacular name for the widespread ragged robin, *Lychnis flos-cuculi*, and is often applied to its close relations, the campions, especially the red, *Silene dioica*, known as Bob Robin, Poor Robin, Red Robin Hood, Robin-in-the-Hedge, Robin's Eye, and similar. Herb robert, *Geranium robertianum,* has a similar list, often with 'little' attached, and 'little robin' has become the standard name for its rare close relative, *Geranium purpureum*. Though these plants have reddish flowers, the colour is different from that of the robin and the only British plant with a similar red to the robin, the poppy, has, as far as I can tell, never had a robin name. Other plant names include Robin-run-the hedge, Robin-run-in-the field and Robin's eye. These apply to widely differing and emphatically non-red plants, such as milkwort, lady's bedstraw, goosegrass, ground-ivy, forget-me-not, and others. There is also the well-known gall on roses, the 'robin's pin-cushion', a growth deformity caused by a small wasp. These must refer to the mischievous Robin Goodfellow, rather than the bird.

The word is used for some other things where the bird is not implied, such as a round-robin letter, and as an early word for a musical round or canon.

MY ACKNOWLEDGEMENTS

The idea for this book initially came when my father stayed with the Rev. J.M. McWilliam in the late 1940s and browsed through his library. In addition, he acknowledged the help of a number of correspondents, most now deceased.

For the present book I had much encouragement, and later critical reading of the text, from my mother, Elizabeth Lack. My publisher, Sandra Saer, also believed in the book from the start and has given much helpful criticism. During the writing, Stewart Beer has sent me the most wonderful stream of messages with references, books from his extensive library, photographs and thoughts. The book has benefited hugely from his contribution.

I am also indebted to Elizabeth North, who has read and criticised the whole book in draft and suggested many improvements. Euan Dunn, in addition to providing the delightful cartoons, made most useful comments on the text. Peter Walton generously sent me his two lovely poetry collections, and Caroline Jackson-Houlston led me to a few poets I might otherwise have missed. Pat and Mary Morris provided my family with warm hospitality, while we were admiring the great tableaux of Walter Potter and Peter Spicer in their home. My wife, Helen, did much of the typing and she and my children have provided all the support anyone could wish for.

Chapter 1

'Tamest of the Feathered Race'

February 1947 was intensely cold, rationing was still in place and Britain was only beginning to recover from the war years. To my father, walking in the woods outside Oxford, the silent, snow-covered landscape seemed to belong to the fifteenth rather than the twentieth century. The stillness was broken with a call of 'Bobby! Bobby!' from an old woman, wrapped in shawls, emerging from a solitary cottage at the edge of a large wood. Scraping aside the fresh snow from a small patch of ground, she scattered her breakfast crumbs, and an expectant robin came down to feed. This friendly action also recalled a much earlier time:

> And when the short days
> > Begin to be cold,
> Robin redbreast will come home to ye,
> > And be very bold.

> Robert Crowley (c.1517-1588), from *Of Flaterars*

That custom started long before this. In *The Parliament of Fowls*, of around 1381, Chaucer gave to each bird its proverbial attribute and here, together with the false lapwing, thieving chough, wedded turtle, wise raven, and many others, is found the 'tame ruddok'. The tameness of the bird, and our kindness towards it, must already have been of long standing by the fourteenth century.

Tributes to the robin come from people in all walks of life; they appear in great poems and nursery rhymes, political diatribes and domestic notebooks. Charmingly, Michael Drayton could not regard the ark as filled until:

> 'The charitable robinet in came, whose nature taught
> the others to be tame.'

> Michael Drayton (1563-1631), *Noah's Flood*

1

Izaak Walton called it:

'Honest robin, that loves mankind both alive and dead.'

Izaak Walton (1593-1683) from *The Compleat Angler*
(1653)

One children's alphabet has:

'R stands for Robin, with waistcoat so smart;
He has found a warm corner in everyone's heart.'

from *An ABC of Birds*
(T. Nelson & Sons, London, undated)

The great political essayist and art critic, William Hazlitt, clearly jaded by some human contacts, was the robin's friend, too:

'Food, warmth, sleep, and a book; these are all I at present ask – the *ultima thule* of my wandering desires. Do you not then wish for

A friend in your retreat,
To whom you may whisper, 'solitude is sweet?'

'Expected, well enough: gone, still better. Such attractions are strengthened by distance. Not a mistress? "Beautiful mask! I know thee!" When I can judge of the heart from the face, of the thoughts from the lips, I may again trust myself. Instead of these, give me the robin redbreast, pecking the crumbs at the door, or warbling on the leafless spray, the same glancing form that has followed me wherever I have been, and "done its spiriting gently".'

William Hazlitt (1778-1830),
from *A Farewell to Essay-Writing*

'Pretty bird, how cheerfully dost thou sit and sing; and yet knowest not where thou art, nor where thou shalt make thy next meal, and at night must shroud thyself in a bush for lodging! What a shame it is for me, that see before me so liberal provisions of my God, and find myself set warm under my own roof; yet am ready to droop in a distrustful and unthankful dullness! Had I so little certainty of my harbour and purveyance, how heartless should I be, how careful! how little list should I have to make music to thee or myself! Surely ... God sent thee, not so much to delight as to shame me.'

Bishop Joseph Hall (1574-1656),
from *Meditations*

'He is determined to engage in social relations ... I did not own the robin – he owned me – or perhaps we owned each other. He was an English robin and he was a <u>person</u> – not a mere bird.'

Frances Hodgson Burnett (1849-1924),
from *My Robin* (1913)

Similar stories come from Scotland. The Scottish conservationist and raconteur, Dr John Berry (1907-2002) of Tayfield, told of how, during the Second World War, an American officer was invited for Christmas to his great Scottish house. The officer was very nervous as to the formalities and, as the grand doorway opened, saw with astonishment, his hostess waving a broom on the stairs. Two robins had taken up territories in the house during a spell of cold weather; at this moment the upstairs robin had trespassed on the territory of the downstairs bird, and the resulting fight had to be broken up.

The earliest reference to the bird's nickname without the redbreast comes from Scotland:

'Robeen and the litil vran var homely in vyntir.'
('Robin and the little wren come to homes in winter.')

Anonymous, from *The Complaynt of Scotland* (1549)

3

The contrast between the French and British attitudes is well shown by the accounts of the robin in two major eighteenth century natural history books, Buffon's *Histoire Naturelle des Oiseaux* (1770-86) and Pennant's *British Zoology* (1766). Buffon was mainly concerned with methods of catching the robin. Pennant, on the other hand, wrote:

> 'This bird, though so very petulant as to be at constant war with its own tribe, yet is remarkably sociable with mankind: in the winter it frequently makes one of the family; and takes refuge from the inclemency of the season even by our fire sides.'

Thomas Pennant (1726-1798),
from *British Zoology* (1776, 4th edn.)

In winter, the robin has found a home not only in the houses of people[1], but the house of God. In churches it has nearly always been welcomed, and there are several stories of it accompanying services and occasionally nesting (see Chapter 8). In the seventeenth century, for instance, Peter du Moulin (1601-1684) commended a robin for its regular attendance at the services in Canterbury Cathedral in a Latin poem. There are several other occurrences (also Chapter 9):

> 'A singular story is told of a robin redbreast, who, for fifteen years[2], inhabited the cathedral of Bristol, and received its subsistence from the hands of the verger. During the time of divine service, it usually perched upon one of the mitres of the organ, and accompanied the solemnity with offering up its harmonious praise.

---

[1]   Robins seem less frequent in houses now than they did forty years ago and earlier. It is still tame and fed with other birds outside, but is it losing its special place as the household bird?

[2]   Fifteen years is unquestionably an exaggeration. Once they have reached adulthood, robins normally live for less than two years, occasionally up to five. In captivity they have lived to 11 years old.

'The following elegant lines were written by a member of that church on this little Chorister:

'Sweet social bird! whose soft harmonious lays
Swell the glad song of the Creator's praise...

[many lines on how safe it is from winter, hawks, schoolboys, then ...]

... Thou, perch'd on high, shall hear th'adoring throng,
Catch the warm strains, and aid the sacred song,
Increase the solemn chorus, and inspire
Each tongue with music, and each heart with fire.'

Joseph Taylor, from *Tales of the Robin* (1815)

5

'A robin redbreast went with us all round [the cloisters of
Winchester College], hopping from opening to opening,
or perching on the bushes near us. "Ay," said the porter,
"that is the chapel robin, it regularly attends service." '

William Howitt,
from *Visits to Remarkable Places* (1840)

'The robin is the only bird which frequents from choice
the inside of churches. Jackdaws resort to the towers, but
that is for safety; owls harbour in the belfry, but that is
for concealment; other birds are sometimes shut into a
church and remain there just because they cannot find
the way out; but to the redbreast a church is a home,
he perches on the columns, roosts on the pillars and
pipes with the organ. He knows his way out, but he is
content to stay. Would he do so if the church were shut
up and deserted? I think not.'

Rev. C.A. Johns,
from *British Birds in their Haunts* (1862)

There are many poems on the robin's tameness, especially in winter.
Here is a selection dating from the early eighteenth century to the
present day:

from Winter

The Fowls of heaven,
Tam'd by the cruel Season, crowd around
The winnowing store, and claim the little boon
Which Providence assigns them. One alone,
The redbreast, sacred to the household gods,
Wisely regardful of the embroiling sky,
In joyless fields and thorny thickets leaves
His shivering mates, and pays to trusted man

His annual visit. Half afraid, he first
Against the window beats; then, brisk, alights
On the warm hearth; then, hopping o'er the floor,
Eyes all the smiling family askance,
And pecks, and starts, and wonders where he is —
Till, more familiar grown, the table crumbs
Attract his slender feet.

James Thomson[3] (1700–1748)

Invitation to the Redbreast

Sweet bird, whom the winter constrains —
   And seldom another it can —
To seek a retreat — while he reigns
   In the well-shelter'd dwellings of man,
Who never can seem to intrude,
   Though in all places equally free,
Come, oft as the season is rude,
   Thou art sure to be welcome to me.

At sight of the first feeble ray,
   That pierces the clouds of the east,
To inveigle thee every day
   My windows shall show thee a feast.
For, taught by experience, I know
   Thee mindful of benefit long;
And that, thankful for all I bestow,
   Thou wilt pay me with many a song.

---

[3]   Thomson was the most highly regarded poet of his day, particularly for his Miltonic epic, *The Seasons*, from which this is extracted. It was the inspiration for Haydn's *Seasons* oratorio and a big influence on John Clare who regarded him, correctly, as our first true pastoral poet. Thomson is now largely ignored except for one, usually unattributed, poem: 'Rule Britannia'.

Then, soon as the swell of the buds
    Bespeaks the renewal of spring,
Fly hence, if thou wilt, to the woods,
    Or where it shall please thee to sing:
And shouldst thou, compell'd by a frost,
    Come again to my window or door,
Doubt not an affectionate host,
    Only pay, as thou pay'dst me before.

Thus music must needs be confest
    To flow from a fountain above;
Else how should it work in the breast
    Unchangeable friendship and love?
And who on the globe can be found,
    Save your generation and ours,
That can be delighted by sound,
    Or boasts any musical powers?

William Cowper (1731-1800)

A Welcome To a Robin Redbreast

Little bird, with bosom red,
Welcome to my humble shed!
Courtly dames of high degree
Have no room for thee and me;
Pride and pleasure's fickle throng
Nothing mind an idle song.
Daily near my table steal,
While I pick my scanty meal;
Doubt not, little though there be,
But I'll cast a crumb to thee;
Well rewarded, if I spy
Pleasure in thy glancing eye;
See thee, when thou'st eat thy fill,
Plume thy breast and wipe thy bill.
Come, my feathered friend, again!

Well thou know'st the broken pane;
Ask of me thy daily store,
Go not near *Avaro's* door;
Once within his iron hall,
Woeful end shall thee befall.
Savage! He would soon divest
Of its rosy plumes thy breast.
Then, with solitary joy,
Eat thee, bones and all, my boy.

John Langhorne (1735-1779)

The Redbreast

Oh Robin, but you're fair forlorn
Your plumes wi' winter war are torn;
The world is white wi' snaw this morn,
      And yet drifts thick;
I ha'e a pickle of groats o' corn
      For you to pick.

Let na mishap your spirits daunt,
I've been mysel' oftimes in want,
And yet my cot the needy haunt,
      Tho' unco bare
And let my meal be e'er sae scant
      I gi'e a share

An' Robin, I'll provide for thee,
Till spring wi' blossoms dress the tree,
And ope the flowrets on the lee,
      Then let thee gang
Back to the grove, where bonnilie
      Ye'll sing your sang

Attributed to Robert Burns (1759-1796), from *The
Robin Redbreast: A New Song Book* (J. Marshall of Newcastle,
1825)

from *To a Redbreast, that Flew in at my Window*

From snowy plains, and icy sprays,
From moonless nights, and sunless days,
Welcome, poor bird! I'll cherish thee;
I love thee, for thou trustest me.
Thrice welcome, helpless, panting guest!
Fondly I'll warm thee in my breast: —
How quick thy little heart is beating!
As if its brother flutterer greeting.
Thou need'st not dread a captive's doom;
No: freely flutter round my room;
Perch on my lute's remaining string,
And sweetly of sweet summer sing.
That note, that summer note, I know;
It wakes at once, and soothes my woe;
I see those woods, I see that stream,
I see, — ah, still prolong the dream!
Still with thy song those scenes renew,
Though through my tears they reach my view.

James Grahame (1765–1811)

The Redbreast (lines suggested in a Westmorland cottage)

Driven in by autumn's sharpening air
From half-striped woods and pastures bare,
Brisk Robin seeks a kindlier home:
Not like a beggar is he come,
But enters as a looked-for guest
Confiding in his ruddy breast,
As if it were a natural shield
Charged with a blazon on the field,
Due to that good and pious deed
Of which we in the Ballad read.

But pensive fancies putting by,
And wild-wood sorrows, speedily
He plays the expert ventriloquist;
And, caught by glimpses now – now missed,
Puzzles the listener with a doubt
If the soft voice he throws about
Comes from within doors or without!
Was ever such a sweet confusion,
Sustained by delicate illusion?
He's at your elbow – to your feeling
The notes are from the floor or ceiling;
And there's a riddle to be guessed,
Till you have marked his heaving chest,
And busy throat whose sink and swell,
Betray the Elf that loves to dwell
In Robin's bosom, as a chosen cell.

William Wordsworth (1770-1850)

In explanation of this poem, Wordsworth wrote:

> 'Our cats having been banished the house, it was soon frequented by redbreasts. Two or three of them, when the window was open, would come in, particularly when Mary was breakfasting alone, and hop about the table picking up the crumbs. My sister being then confined to her room by sickness, as, dear creature, she still is, had one that, without being caged, took up its abode with her, and at night used to perch upon a nail from which a picture had hung. It used to sing and fan her face with its wings in a manner that was very touching.'

From The Prose Works of William Wordsworth,
ed. by A.B. Grosart (1876)

Wild Redbreast! hadst thou at Jemima's lip
Pecked, as at mine, thus boldly, Love might say,
A half-blown rose had tempted thee to sip
Its glistening dews; but hallowed is the clay
Which the Muse warms; and I, whose head is grey,
Am not unworthy of thy fellowship;
Nor could I let one thought – one notion – slip
That might thy sylvan confidence betray.
For are we not all His without whose care
Vouchsafed no sparrow falleth to the ground?
Who gives his Angels wings to speed through air,
And rolls the planets through the blue profound;
Then peck or perch, fond Flutterer! nor forbear
To trust a Poet in still musings bound.

William Wordsworth (1827)

John Clare in 1809, aged 16, writes with feeling about different
attitudes towards the robin:

from *The Robin*

Now the snow hides the ground, little birds leave the wood,
And fly to the cottage to beg for their food;
While the robin, domestic, more tame than the rest,
With its wings drooping down, and rough feathers undrest,
Comes close to our windows, as much as to say,
'I would venture in, if I could find a way:
I'm starv'd, and I want to get out of the cold;
Oh! Make me a passage, and think me not bold.'
....
Come in, and a welcome reception thou'lt find;
I keep no grimalkin to murder inclin'd.
But oh, little robin! Be careful to shun
That house, where the peasant makes use of a gun;

For if thou but taste of the seed he has strew'd,
Thy life as a ransom must pay for the food:

John Clare (1793-1864)

from *The Woodman*

The robin tamest of the feathered race
Soon as he hears the woodman sounding chops
Wi' ruddy bosom and a simple face
Around his old companion's feet he hops
And there for hours in pleas'd attention stops
The woodman's heart is tender and humane
And at his meals he many a crumble drops,
Thanks to thy generous feelings gentle swain
And what thy pity gives shall not be gave in vain.

John Clare

from *Winter*

And little birds with hunger tame
To cottage yards undaunted go
Where pity warms some gentle dame
To scatter crumbles round the snow

Yet all save robins will retreat
And shun rude mans forbidding sight
Who seemly welcomes trampling feet
And ruffs his feathers in delight
Brisk hopping from the shielding thorn
As one who would our steps detain
Then droops its wing and sits forlorn
When left to solitude again

John Clare

13

I love to hear the evening crows go bye
And see the starnels darken down the sky
The bleaching stack the bustling sparrow leaves
And plops with merry note beneath the eaves
The odd and lated pigeon bounces bye
As if a wary watching hawk was nigh
While far and fearing nothing high and low
The stranger birds to distant places go
While short of flight the evening robin comes
To watch the maiden sweeping out the crumbs
Nor fears the idle shout of passing boy
But pecks about the door and sings for joy
Then in the hovel where the cows are fed
Finds till the morning comes a pleasant bed.

John Clare, from *The Northborough Sonnets*

from *To a Robin Red-breast*

… In stately hall and rustic dome,
     The gaily robed and homely poor
Will watch the hour when thou shall come,
     And bid thee welcome to the door.

The Herdsman on the upland hill,
     The Ploughman in the hamlet near,
Are prone thy little paunch to fill,
     And pleased thy little psalm to hear.

Nor are thy little wants forgot
     In Beggar's hut or Crispin's stall;
The Miser only feeds thee not,
     Who suffers ne'er a crumb to fall.

The Youth who strays, with dark design,
     To make each well-stored nest a prey,

If dusky hues denote them thine,
    Will draw his pilfering hand away.

The Peacock's plumes in pride may swell,
    The Parrot prate eternally,
But yet no bird man loves so well,
    As thou with thy simplicity.

John Jones, c. 1827⁴

from *The Months*

January

Cold the day and cold the drifted snow,
Dim the day until the cold dark night.
Crackle, sparkle, faggot; embers glow:
Someone may be plodding through the snow
Longing for a light,

For the light that you and I can show,
If no-one else should come.
Here Robin Redbreast's welcome to a crumb,
And never troublesome:
Robin, why don't you come and fetch your crumb?
Here's butter for my hunch of bread,
    And sugar for your crumb;
Here's room upon the hearthrug,
    If you'll only come.

In your scarlet waistcoat,
    With your keen bright eye,

---

⁴   This poem, 13 verses in all, was sent by John Jones to the poet laureate Robert Southey. John Jones was the uneducated butler of Kirby Hall. The poem, in particular, and the poet's dedicated life, clearly affected Southey who expressed himself 'pleased at seeing how much intellectual enjoyment had been attained in humble life' and got this and other poems of Jones published.

Where are you loitering?
　　Wings were made to fly!

Make haste to breakfast,
　　Come and fetch your crumb,
For I'm as glad to see you
　　As you are glad to come.

Christina Rossetti (1830–1894)

'The birds were silent – and even robin redbreast, whose chirruping song was heard among the bushes near the Lodge, emboldened by the largesses with which the good old knight always encouraged his familiarity, did not venture into the recesses of the wood, where he encountered the sparrowhawk, and other enemies of a similar description, preferring the vicinity of the dwellings of man, from whom he, almost solely among the feathered tribes, seems to experience disinterested protection.'

from *Woodstock*, Sir Walter Scott (1771–1832)

Address to a Robin

Come, sweetest of the feathered throng,
And soothe me with thy plaintive song;
Come to my cot, devoid of fear,
No danger shall await thee here:
No prowling cat, with whiskered face,
Approaches this sequestered place:
No schoolboy with his willow bow
Shall aim at thee a murderous blow;
No wily limed twig molest
Thy olive wing or crimson breast:
Thy cup, sweet bird! I'll daily fill

At yonder cressy, bubbling rill;
Thy board shall plenteously be spread
With crumblets of the nicest bread.
And when rude winter comes, and shows
His icicles and shivering snows,
Hop o'er my cheering hearth, and be
One of my peaceful family
Then soothe me with thy plaintive song,
Thou sweetest of the feathered throng!

Edward Jenner (1749-1823)[5]

The next poem is unusual, being written in Yorkshire dialect. F.W. Moorman had collected dialect poems and then wrote some himself, despite describing himself as a 'bourgeois professor' (of English Literature, at Leeds):

The Gardener and the Robin

Why! Bobbie, so thou's coom agean!
    I'm fain to see thee here;
It's lang sin I've set een on thee,
    It's ommost hauf a yeer.
What's that thou says? Thou's taen a wife
    An' raised a family.
It seems thou's gien 'em all the slip
    Now back-end's drawin' nigh.

I mun forgi'e thee; we're owd friends,
    An' fratchin's not for us;
Blackbirds an' spinks[6] I can't abide,
    At doves an' crows I cuss.

---

[5] Perhaps not the most distinguished of poems here, but Edward Jenner was the inventor of vaccination, and 'in the intervals of practice, made botanical and ornithological observations, collected fossils, played on the flute and violin, and wrote occasional poems'. He was the first to show that cuckoos eject the eggs or young of their foster parents – a story at first widely disbelieved.

[6] Chaffinches

But thou'll noan steal my strawberries,
    Or nip my buds o' plum;
Most feather-fowl I drive away,
    But thou can awlus coom.

Ay, that's thy place, at top o' t' clod,
    Thy heead cocked o' one side,
Lookin' as far-learnt as a judge.
    Is that a worm thou's spied?
By t'Megs: he's well-nigh six inch lang,
    An' reed as t' gate i' t' park;
If thou don't mesh him up a bit,
    He'll gie thee belly-wark.

My missus awlus lets me know
    I'm noan so despert thin;
If I ate sausages as thou
    Eats worms, I'd brust my skin!
How'd on! Leave soom for t' mowdiwarps[7]
    That scrats down under t' grund;
Of worms, an' mawks[8], and bummel-clocks[9]
    Thou's etten hauf a pund.

So now thou'll clear thy pipes and sing:
    Grace after meat, I s'pose.
Thou looks as holy as t'owd saint
    In church wi' broken nose.
Thou's plannin' marlocks[10] all the time,
    Donned i' thy sowdier coat;
An' what we tak for hymns o' praise
    Is just thy fratchin' note.

---

[7]   moles
[8]   maggots
[9]   beetles
[10] tricks

I've seen thee feightin' theer on t'lawn,
 Beneath yon laurel tree;
Thy neb was reed wi' blooid, thou looked
 As chuffy as could be.
Thou's got no mense nor morals, Bob,
 But weel I know thy charm.
Ay, thou can stand upon my spade.
 I'll niver do thee harm.

  F.W. Moorman (1872-1919), from *Songs of the Ridings* (c. 1900)

In the early twentieth century there was a flowering of interest in natural history generally and, with it, a small flurry of books, many of them with personal, sentimental anecdotes about the robin's tameness. By contrast, most poets of the last hundred years refer to other aspects, perhaps taking their tameness as simply understood, though it is specifically mentioned occasionally:

from *The Hon. Sec.*[11]

The flag that hung half-mast today
Seemed animate with being
As if it knew for whom it flew
And will no more be seeing ...

He died when early April light
Showed red his garden sally
And under pale green spears glowed white
His lilies of the valley:

That garden where he used to stand
And where the robin waited
To fly and perch upon his hand
And feed till it was sated.

---

[11] I have omitted verses 2-6

The Times would never have the space
For Ned's discreet achievements,
The public prints are not the place
For intimate bereavements.

A gentle guest, a willing host,
Affection deeply planted –
It's strange that those we miss the most
Are those we take for granted.

John Betjeman (1906-1984), from *High and Low* (1966)

Robin

When wind brings more snow
To deepen deep snow

Robin busies his beak.
But the pickings are bleak.

He stands at the open door
Asking for more.

'Anything edible?'
He stares towards the table.

The cat can't believe
A bird could be so naïve.

Half-shut eye, wide ear
She prays: 'Let him come near!'

Then, with his flaming shirt
Telling him nothing can hurt,

And that he will always win,
Robin bounces in.

Ted Hughes (1930-1998), from *The Iron Wolf* (1995)

Encounter With An Old Robin

This morning, raining,
he came into the kitchen,
moved around, slowly,
swivelling his head
in a total circle,
the way birds can.

Glazed, half-closed eyes
and matted, shaggy feathers
proclaimed his age.
His faded breast
was the red of
'Old MacGregor' tartan.

I was trying to eat.
No matter.
This was a situation I had to meet,
there and then.

'Come on,' I said,
'come out!'
(A perk of the ruffled head.)
'You need to eat.'

Beyond the cottage door
I threw some seed.
Reluctantly, the robin
left the warmth of the kitchen
and stood beside me,
considering the meal…

Next time I went out
The seed still lay, untouched,
on the damp ground.
There was no sign of him.

Friendship appears
in all shapes and sizes.

Watersfield, 2007   Sandra MacGregor Hastie

To finish this chapter, here is the earliest reference to a tame robin
that I know of.

St. Kentigern, later known as Mungo (literally 'darling'), was a pupil
of Serf at Culross in Fife at the time of this incident. He was ordained
bishop in c.540 A.D. and founded Glasgow Cathedral. He died in
603. This association has led to the earliest known illustration of a
robin, on the episcopal seal of Robert Wyschard, bishop of Glasgow
in 1272. Since then it has featured on the Glasgow coat-of-arms. It

is referred to in a hymn in the *Missa Sancti Kentigerni* of 1492 and in the second lesson of the service for St. Kentigern in the Aberdeen Breviary of 1509-10.

Of the little bird which was killed and then restored to life by Kentigern

'The fellow pupils of St. Kentigern, seeing that he was loved by their teacher and spiritual father (Serf) more than all the rest, hated him, nor could they say anything peaceably to him either publicly or in private. Wherefore in many ways they lay in wait for him, abused, envied, and slandered him. But the child of the Lord always had the eyes of his heart towards the Lord, and grieved more for them than for himself, caring little for all the unjust machinations of men. Now, a little bird, which on account of the redness of its body is called the redbreast, by the will of the Heavenly Father, without whom not one sparrow falleth to the ground, was wont to receive its daily food from the hand of Serf, the servant of God, and in consequence of this had become familiar and at home with him. Sometimes it was even wont to rest upon his head, or face, or shoulder, or in his bosom, or to sit by his side as he prayed or read; and by the flapping of its wings, or by the sound of its inarticulate voice, or by some other little gesture, it showed the affection which it had for him. So that sometimes the face of the man of God assumed the joy which was shadowed forth in the motion of the bird, as he wondered at the great power of the Creator in this little creature, to Whom the dumb speak, and irrational things are known to have understanding.

'And because this bird, frequently, at the command or beck of the man of God, came to him or departed from him, it brought to light the unbelief and hardness of heart of his disciples, and showed clearly their disobedience. Let not this seem strange to anyone, seeing that the Lord, by the voice of an animal dumb and a beast of burden, reproved the foolishness of the prophet; and Solomon, the wisest of men, sends the sluggard to the ant, that, by considering its labour and industry, he may shake off his torpor and sloth. Moreover, a holy and wise man called his religious to consider the work of the bees, that in their little bodies they might learn the beautiful discipline of service. But perhaps it will seem marvellous to some that a man so holy and perfect should take delight in the play or ways of a little bird. But let such know that perfect men ought at times to have the severity of their discipline mitigated by something of this kind, in order that they who mentally rise up to God may at times lower themselves to us; because even the bow requires occasionally to be unbent from its daily strain, lest at the needful time it be found nerveless and useless for the discharge of the arrow. For birds in passing through the air rise with outstretched wings, and again closing them, descend to the lower parts of the earth.

'Therefore on a certain day, when the aged man entered his oratory to offer up to God the incense of prayers, the boys took advantage of his absence, and began to indulge in play with the aforesaid little bird; and, while they handled it among themselves, and tried to snatch it from each other, it died in their hands, and its head was torn from its body. When this was done their play was changed into sorrow, and they already in imagination saw the strokes of the rods, which are wont to be the greatest torment of boys, hanging over them. At length, having taken counsel among themselves, they laid the blame on the boy Kentigern, who had kept himself entirely aloof from the affair, and they showed him the dead bird, and threw it from them before the old man arrived. The old man took the destruction of the bird very ill, and threatened to avenge its death on its destroyer very severely. The boys, therefore, rejoiced, thinking that they had escaped, and that they had turned on Kentigern the punishment due to themselves, and that they had lessened the grace of friendship which Serf had hitherto entertained towards him.

'When Kentigern, the most pure child, learned this, he took the bird into his hands, put the head to the body, and impressed upon it the sign of the cross, and raising his pure hands in prayer to the Lord, said: "O Lord Jesus Christ, in whose hands is the breath of all Thy creatures, rational and irrational, give back to this little bird the breath of life, that Thy blessed name be glorified for ever." These words spake the Saint in prayer, and immediately the bird was restored to life; and not only rose safely with untramelled flight in the air, but flew forth in its usual way to meet the old man with joy as he returned from the church. On seeing this prodigy the heart of the holy old man exulted in the Lord, and his soul magnified the child of the Lord in the Lord, and the Lord who alone doeth marvellous works, and was working in the child. By this remarkable sign, therefore, the Lord signified, nay, in a way presignified, Kentigern to be His own, and began to announce him whom He afterwards, and in manifold ways, made more remarkable by wonders.'

Translated from the twelfth-century account of Jocelin, a monk of Furness, by W.M. Metcalfe, *Ancient Lives of the Scottish Saints* (1895). Jocelin is said to have used an account by St. Kentigern's disciple, St. Asaph

Left: A seal from 17th century including the Glasgow coat of arms. The tree on which the robin is perched is a late addition

Right: The seal of Robert Wyschard, Bishop of Glasgow, 13th century

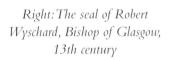

Chapter 2

The Saga of Cock Robin

The oldest known printed version of the anonymous *Who killed Cock Robin?* was intended for children. It is a small chap-book[12] now in the British Museum, dating from the early 1700s. Unusually for children's literature of the time, it has no obvious moral, indeed no point at all that anyone can now see. Most tales and verses written specially for children have only a temporary popularity, but this one - a simple and abrupt tale of blood and funeral rites - has survived and is now seen as more of a traditional nursery rhyme. It has a much wider distribution than the bird which it celebrates, as it is known across the English-speaking world with some minor variations.

The poem itself is probably much older than 1700 and not written in the first place for children. E. A. Armstrong in *The Folklore of the Birds* (1958) suggests that a fifteenth-century stained glass window at Buckland Rectory, Gloucester, depicts a robin pierced with an arrow. It may have originated through allusions to medieval symbolism or pagan ceremonies, but if so there is no clear idea what they were. By now there is doubt even as to the correct symbols, e.g., the 'beadle' is sometimes depicted as an officer of the law and sometimes as a beetle; the bull who could pull must be an ox, but some have supposed that it was a bullfinch, popular as a cage-bird; and when did the link between 'lark' and 'clerk' originate and when did it start singing 'Amen' as in the companion nursery-rhyme of *The Marriage of Cock Robin and Jenny Wren?*[13] In addition for 'shovel' to rhyme with 'owl' it needs the archaic form 'showl'.

---

[12]   Chap-books, or 'penny-dreadfuls' to the literary establishment, were pocket-sized pamphlets usually of less than 20 pages, printed and sold cheaply and with no cover. They originally peddled subversive ideas but quickly adapted for children's books, poetry, serialisations, etc.

[13]   There is a parallel with Herrick (1591-1674): 'Sweet singing lark Be thou the clerk, And know thy when To say, Amen.' suggesting that he knew the rhymes.

Pictures have often accompanied the story. In the first half of the nineteenth century some were beautifully coloured by hand and Thomas Bewick designed a set of illustrations. Later in the nineteenth century the standard fell with cheap colour reproduction. The poem itself was often modified, e.g. in one garish edition, of 1879, the 'death' was depicted in the grounds of the Crystal Palace, and the tale was extended to fit the new surroundings. Probably the most remarkable illustration that the poem has received is not in a book at all. In 1861 Walter Potter set out a 'tableau' of the story in no fewer than 98 stuffed specimens plus insects and background that had taken him seven years to compile. This, one of the best-known of all examples of Victorian taxidermy, was on display in his native village of Bramber in Sussex for many years. It is now in private hands, though displayed at intervals. Some other taxidermists took up the story in a smaller way, e.g. Peter Spicer.

There is a companion rhyme to the *Death*. *The Marriage of Cock Robin and Jenny Wren* was usually printed in front of it in the late eighteenth and early nineteenth centuries. It has been suggested that *The Marriage* was a late and spurious addition to *The Death*, especially as it shows that the death was accidental, and that the sparrow had good intentions. But this is unproven and both themes are common enough in folk-lore, where they also appear in various other forms. Here, then, are both rhymes as they would have been read by a child at the beginning of the nineteenth century.

Further rhymes, quoted here, follow up the themes. Such survivals support the idea that an ancient and widespread but now forgotten rite lies behind these simple rhymes – a pleasing mystery, and one that is unlikely ever to be solved.

The Marriage of Cock Robin and Jenny Wren

It was on a merry time,
When Jenny Wren was young,
So neatly as she danced,
And so sweetly as she sung.

Robin Redbreast lost his heart,
He was a gallant bird;
He doffed his hat to Jenny,
And thus to her he said:

'My dearest Jenny Wren,
If you will but be mine,
You shall dine on cherry-pie
And drink currant-wine.

I'll dress you like a Goldfinch,
Or like a Peacock gay;
So if you'll have me, Jenny,
Let us appoint the day.'

Jenny blushed behind her fan,
And thus declared her mind:
'Then let it be tomorrow, Bob, –
I take your offer kind.

'Cherry-pie is very good!
So is currant-wine!
But I will wear my brown gown,
And never dress too fine.'

Robin rose up early,
At the break of day;
He flew to Jenny Wren's house,
To sing a roundelay.

He met the Cock and Hen,
And bid the Cock declare
This was his wedding-day
With Jenny Wren the fair.

The Cock then blew his horn,
To let the neighbours know
This was Robin's wedding-day,
And they might see the show.

And first came Parson Rook,
With his spectacles and band;
And one of Mother Hubbard's books
He held within his hand.

Then followed him the Lark
For he could sweetly sing,
And he was to be clerk
At Cock Robin's wedding.

He sang of Robin's love
For little Jenny Wren,
And when he came unto the end
Then he began again.

Then came the Bride and Bridegroom;
Quite plainly she was dressed,
And blushed so her cheek was
As red as Robin's breast.

But Robin cheered her up;
And said, 'My pretty Jen
We're going to be married,
And marriage is no sin.'

The Goldfinch he came next,
To give away the bride;
The Linnet, being bridesmaid,
Walked by Jenny's side;

And as she was a-walking,
Said, 'Upon my word,
I think that your Cock Robin
Is a very pretty bird!'

The Bullfinch walked by Robin,
And thus to him did say,
'Pray mark, friend Robin Redbreast
That Goldfinch dressed so gay;

'What though her gay apparel
Becomes her very well,
Yet Jenny's modest dress and look
Must bear away the bell.'

The Blackbird and the Thrush,
And charming Nightingale,
Whose sweet jug sweetly echoes
Through every grove and dale;

The Sparrow and Tom Tit,
And many more, was there:
All for to see the wedding
Of Jenny Wren the fair.

'Oh, then' says Parson Rook,
'Who gives this maid away?'
'I do,' says the Goldfinch,
'And her fortune I will pay:

'Here's a bag of grain of many sorts,
And other things beside;
Now happy be the Bridegroom,
And happy be the Bride!'

'And will you have her, Robin,
To be your wedded wife?'
'Yes, I will,' says Robin,
'And love her all my life.'

'And will you have him, Jenny,
Your husband now to be?'
'Yes, I will,' says Jenny,
'And love him heartily.'

Then on her finger fair
Cock Robin put the ring;
'You're married now', says Parson Rook;
While the Lark amen did sing:

'Happy be the Bridegroom,
And happy be the bride!
And may not man, nor bird, nor beast,
This happy pair divide.'

The birds were asked to dine;
Nor were the birds alone,
But many a pretty beast
That had Cock Robin known.

They had cherry-pie,
Besides some currant-wine.
And every guest brought something
That sumptuous they might dine.

Now they all sat or stood,
To eat and to drink;
And everyone said what
They happened to think.

And when they'd done eating,
They each took a noggin,
To Jenny the Bride, and the
Bridegroom Cock Robin.

The dinner things moved,
They began for to sing;
And they all made the place
Near a mile round to ring.

The concert was fine;
And every bird tried
Who should sing best for Robin
And Jenny Wren the Bride.

When in came the Cuckoo,
And made a great rout;
He caught hold of Jenny,
And pulled her about.

Cock Robin was angry,
And so was the Sparrow,
Who now is preparing his
Bow and his arrow.

His aim then he took,
But he took it not right;
His skill it was bad,
Or he shot in a fright;

For the Cuckoo he missed,
But Cock Robin he killed!
And all the birds mourned
That his blood was so spilled.

1. *The Marriage of Cock Robin and Jenny Wren,*
from a chap-book of the early nineteenth century

2. '*Who killed Cock Robin?*' case with stuffed specimens by Peter Spicer, c.1870
photo by AL with thanks to Pat and Mary Morris

3. '*Who killed Cock Robin?*' by Walter Potter including 98 stuffed birds, 1861
4. Below: detail from the tableau including most of the birds mentioned in the
rhyme plus the beetle and fly Photos by AL with thanks to Pat and Mary Morris

Who killed Cock Robin?
  I said the Sparrow,
  With my bow and arrow,
And I killed Cock Robin.

Who did see him die?
  I, said the Fly,
  With my little eye,
And I saw him die.

Who catched his blood?
  I, said the Fish,
  With my little dish,
And I catched his blood.

Who made his shroud?
  I, said the Beetle,
  With my little needle,
And I made his shroud.

Who shall dig his grave?
  I, says the Owl,
  With my spade and showl,
And I will dig his grave.

Who will be the parson?
  I, says the Rook,
  With my little book,
And I will be the parson.

Who will be the clerk?
  I, says the Lark,
  If 'tis not in the dark,
And I will be the clerk.

Who'll carry him to the grave?
  I, says the Kite,
  If 'tis not in the night,
And I'll carry him to the grave.

Who will carry the link?
  I, says the Linnet,
  I'll fetch it in a minute,
And I will carry the link.

Who will be chief mourner?
  I, says the Dove,
  For I mourn for my love,
And I'll be the chief mourner.

Who will bear the pall?
  We, says the Wren,
  Both the cock and the hen,
And we will bear the pall.

Who will sing a psalm?
  I, says the Thrush,
  As she sat in a bush,
And I will sing a psalm.

Who will toll the bell?
  I, says the Bull,
  Because I can pull,
And so Cock Robin farewell.

All the birds of the air
  Fell to sighing and sobbing
  When they heard the bell toll
For poor Cock Robin.

Early chap-book editions were often accompanied by other rhymes and these could be rather crude:

> Little robin redbreast
> Sat upon a pole.
> Wiggle waggle went his tail,
> Pop went his hole.

Inevitably, this was cleaned up in the nineteenth century:

> Little robin redbreast
> Sat upon a rail;
> Niddle noddle went his head,
> Wiggle waggle went his tail.

One twentieth-century commentator on the *Death* is worth quoting, both because of his own merits as a poet and for his entertaining descriptions. W.H. Davies in his book, *My Birds*, 1933, has a chapter on the robin which includes:

'Only once in all my life have I read anything by Anon. and been disappointed. It was when I read his immortal poem called *Who Killed Cock Robin?* This poem is so full of errors, where poetry makes no attempt to reconcile itself to truth, that I have come to the conclusion that it was a Saturday night's effusion, when the master was the worse for drink. Take this verse for instance:

> Who'll dig his grave?
> I, said the Owl,
> With my spade and shovel –
> I'll dig his grave.

'What was Anon. thinking of when he wrote that? He did not seem to know that the Mole was a professional digger... and it was the Mole, not the Owl, who never digs, that should have volunteered to have 'dug the hole'.'

Later:

> 'The first verse fills us with something like indignation…
> who ever heard of a Robin being killed by a Sparrow!
> The robin is, for his weight and size, the greatest little
> fighter that ever broke bread or breathed the breath
> of life; and if he was killed at all it must have been by
> another Cock Robin, but a Sparrow – never!'

W. H. Davies (1871-1940)

There is more in similar vein.

Here are two Scottish rhymes relating to the marriage:

> The robin redbreast and the wran
> Coost out about the parritch pan;
> And ere the robin got a spune
> The wran she had the parritch dune.

> The wren she lyes in care's bed,
> In meikle dule and pyne, O.
> When in cam robin redbreist
> Wi' succar-saps and wine, O.
> Now, maiden will ye taste o' this?
> 'Tis succar-saps and wine, O
> Na, ne'er a drap, Robin,
> Though it were ne'er so fine, O.
> And where's the ring that I gied ye;
> Ye little cutty quean[14], O?
> I gied it till an ox-ee [15],
> A kind sweit-heart o'myne, O.

There were more elaborate versions with extra characters, often illustrated, including several versions of the following tale. This one was told by Robert Burns to his younger sister:

Robin's Yule Song

> There was an auld Poussie Baudrons, and she gaed awa'
> down by a waterside, and there she saw a wee Robin
> Redbreast happin' on a brier; and Poussie Baudrons says,
> 'Where's tu gaun, wee Robin?' and wee Robin says, 'I'm
> gaun awa' to the King to sing him a sang this guid Yule

---

[14] short skirt
[15] great tit

morning', and Poussie Baudrons says, 'Come here, wee Robin, and I'll let ye see a bonny white ring round my neck.' But wee Robin says, 'Na, na! gray Poussie Baudrons, na, na! Ye worry't the wee Mousie; but ye'll no worry me.' So wee Robin flew awa' till he came to a fail fauld-dike, and there he saw a gray greedy gled[16] sitting. And gray greedy gled says 'Where's tu gaun, wee Robin? and wee Robin says, 'I'm gaun awa' to the King to sing him a sang this guid Yule morning', and gray greedy gled says, 'Come here, wee Robin, and I'll let ye see a bonny feather in my wing.' But wee Robin says, 'Na, na! gray greedy gled; na, na! Ye pookit a' the wee lintie[17]; but ye'se no pook me.' So wee Robin flew awa' till he came to the chleuch o' a craig, and there he saw slee Tod Lowrie[18] sitting, and slee Tod Lowrie says, 'Where's tu gaun, wee Robin?' and wee Robin says, 'I'm gaun awa' to the King to sing him a sang this guid Yule morning', and Slee Tod Lowrie says, 'Come here, wee Robin, and I'll let ye see a bonny spot on the tap o' my tail.' But wee Robin says, 'Na, na! slee Tod Lowrie, na, na! Ye worry't the wee lammie; but ye'se no worry me.' So wee Robin flew awa' till he came to a bonny burnside, and there he saw a wee callant[19] sitting, and the wee callant says, 'Where's tu gaun, wee Robin?' and wee Robin says, 'I'm gaun awa' to the King, to sing him a sang this guid Yule morning.' And the wee callant says, 'Come here, wee Robin, and I'll gie ye a wheen grand moolins out o' my pooch.' But wee Robin says, 'Na, na! wee callant, na, na! Ye speldert the gowdspink[20], but ye'se ne spelder me!'

---

[16] bird of prey, usually a kite
[17] linnet
[18] fox
[19] boy
[20] goldfinch

So wee Robin flew awa' till he came to the king: and there he sat on a winnock sole, and sang the king a bonny sang. And the king says to the queen, 'What'll we gie to wee Robin for singing us this bonny sang?' And the queen says to the king, 'I think we'll gie him the wee wran, to be his wife.' So wee Robin and the wee wran were married, and the king, and the queen and a' the court danced at the waddin'; syne he flew awa' hame to his ain waterside and happit on a brier.

Robert Burns (1759-1796)

There is an English rhyme about the sick wren (sometimes in a longer version):

The Life and Death of Jenny Wren

Jenny Wren fell sick
  Upon a merry time,
In came Robin Redbreast,
  And brought her sops and wine.

'Eat well of the sops, Jenny,
  Drink well of the wine,'
'Thank you, Robin, kindly;
  You shall be mine.'

Jenny she got well,
  And stood upon her feet,
And told Robin plainly
  She loved him not a bit.

Robin being angry,
  Hopped upon a twig,
Saying, 'Out upon you,
  Fie upon you, bold-faced jig!'

The next rhyme was found surviving as a children's round-game, in the mid-nineteenth century.

> Cock Robin is dead and gone to his grave,
> H'm, haw, gone to his grave,
> Cock Robin is dead and gone to his grave,
> H'm, haw, gone to his grave.
>
> There grew an old apple-tree over his head,
> H'm, haw, etc.
>
> The apples were ripe and they all fell down,
> H'm, haw, etc.
>
> There came an old woman a-picking 'em up,
> H'm, haw, etc.
>
> Old Robin arose and gave her a knock,
> H'm, haw, etc.
>
> Which made the old woman go hippity hop,
> H'm, haw, etc.

The following 'testament', from Scotland, one of several versions, may originate as part of a Yule festival, or similar (Chapter 7). It is full of other allusions:

The Robin's Testament

> Guid-day now, bonnie Robin
>   How lang have you been here?
> I've been a bird about this bush
>   This mair than twenty year.

But now I am the sickest bird
   That ever sat on brier;
And I wad make my testament,
   Guidman, if you wad hear.

'Gar tak this bonnie neb[21] o' mine,
   That picks upon the corn,
And gie't to the Duke o' Hamilton
   To be a hunting horn.

'Gar tak these bonnie feathers o' mine,
   The feathers o' my neb,
And gie to the Lady o' Hamilton
   To fill a feather-bed.[22]

'Gar tak this guid right leg o' mine
   And mend the brig o' Tay[23];
It will be a post and pillar guid,
   It will neither bow nor gae.

'And tak this other leg o' mine
   And mend the brig o' Weir;
It will be a post and pillar guid,
   It'll neither bow nor steer.

'Gar tak these bonnie feathers o' mine
   The feathers o' my tail,
And gie to the lads o' Hamilton
   To be a barn flail.

---

[21] Beak

[22] This and the previous verse must refer to the affair between Nelson and Lady Hamilton.

[23] The Tay Bridge collapsed in 1879, dating the poem to the late 19th century. Did the Brig o' Weir also collapse then? This must refer to the Renfrewshire village, west of Glasgow.

'Gar tak these bonnie feathers o' mine
    The feathers o' my breast
And gie to ony bonnie lad
    That'll bring to me a priest.'

Now in there came my Lady Wren
    With mony a sigh and groan;
'O what care I for a' the lads
    If my wee lad be gone?'

The Robin turned him round about,
    E'en like a little king,
'Go, pack ye out at my chamber door,
    Ye little cutty quean.'

Robin made his testament
    Upon a coll of hay
And by came a greedy gled
    And snapt him a' away.

The *Death* has received allusions from some twentieth-century poets such as Walter de la Mare:

from *The Feather* (1941)

A feather, a feather! –
I wonder whether
Of Wren? Or Sparrow?
Or poor Cock Robin,
Shot with an arrow?

Walter de la Mare (1873-1956)

The robin's death finds some memorials in later times. Four epitaphs were included by Joseph Taylor in his *Tales of the Robin*, in 1815. A quote from two will give a flavour:

from *Epitaph on a Robin*

...They mourned his fall with many a pensive tear
And bade his lov'd remains find shelter here.
And oft, at fading hour of eve they'll bring
The infant treasures of the opening spring;
The woodbine here in Nature's grace shall bloom,
Waving in wild luxuriance o'er his tomb;
The soft-ey'd daisy lends its modest dyes,
To consecrate the turf where Robin lies....

Another: 'Mary and the Robin, a beautiful little Tale by Wm Upton, Esq.,' in eleven verses, relates:

> ...Sweet Robin, e'er constant and true
> Came, as usual, his mistress to meet;
> He came, - to her cold bosom flew!
> And at morn was found dead at her feet...

The Robin's Jubilee of 1826 includes, among others, the following epitaph:

Inscription on a Robin[24]

To the pleasing memory
Of a sweet little songster,
Who possessed qualities
That engaged the beneficent mind;
And though a captive,
Bore his lot like a true philosopher –
For it neither strove,
Nor vented its rage;
And though by hope forsaken,
Was by love cherished.

---

[24] 'Dick' was usually a sparrow and, though it is possible that it originally commemorated a sparrow, not a robin, a sparrow is not a songster

But as fate controls all living creatures,
As there is a time even when kings must die –
So it was with little Dick;
For neither his beauty nor his sprightly notes
Could stop the sable hand of death.
He was buried by pity
Under a currant-tree,
And is remembered with sorrow.

Here are six other poems on the death of the robin:

Epitaph on a Free but Tame Redbreast

These are not dewdrops, these are tears
 And tears by Sally shed
For absent Robin, who, she fears
 With too much cause, is dead.

One morn he came not to her hand
 As he was wont to come,
And, on her finger perched, to stand
 Picking his breakfast-crumb.

Alarmed she called him, and perplexed
 She sought him, but in vain-
That day he came not, nor the next,
 Nor ever came again.

She therefore raised him here a tomb,
 Though where he fell, or how,
None knows, so secret was his doom,
 Nor where he moulders now.

Had half a score of coxcombs died
 In social Robin's stead,
Poor Sally's tears had soon been dried,
 Or haply never shed.

But Bob was neither rudely bold
 Nor spiritlessly tame;
Nor was, like theirs, his bosom cold,
 But always in a flame.

William Cowper (1731–1800)

An Epitaph on a Robin Redbreast

(Inscribed on an Urn in the flower-garden at Hafod.)

Tread lightly here, for here, 'tis said,
When piping winds are hushed around,
A small note wakes from under ground,
Where now his tiny bones are laid.
No more in lone and leafless groves,
With ruffled wing and faded breast,
His friendless, homeless spirit roves;
Gone to the world where birds are blest!
Where never cat glides o'er the green,
Or school-boy's giant form is seen;
But love, and joy, and smiling spring
Inspire their little souls to sing!

Samuel Rogers
(1763 – 1855)

Robin's Cross

A little cross
To tell my loss;
A little bed
To rest my head;
A little tear is all I crave
Under my very little grave.

I strew thy bed
Who loved thy lays;
The tear I shed,
The cross I raise,
With nothing more upon it than –
Here lies the Little Friend of Man!

George Darley (1795 – 1846)

'Out of the Mouths of Babes –'

Two children in my garden playing found
    A robin cruelly dead, in Summer hours.
I watched them get a trowel, and heap the mound,
    And bury him, and scatter over flowers.

And when their little friend was laid away,
    In lack of burial service over the dead
Before those two grave children turned to play:-
    'I hope he'll have a happy *dead* life!' one said.

What more was there to say for bird or beast?
    What more for any man is there to say?
What can we wish *them* better, as with priest
    And choir we ring the cross on Armistice Day?

F.W. Harvey (1888-1957),
from *September and Other Poems* (1925)

47

Snow

Ridges thickly on black bough
  And foaming on twig-fork in swollen lumps
At flirt of bird-wing or wind's sough
  Plump snow tumbled on snow softly with sudden dumps.

Where early steps had made
  A wavering track through the white-blotted road
Breaking its brightness with blue shade,
  Snow creaked beneath my feet with snow heavily shod.

I reached a snow-thatched rick
  Where men sawed bedding off for horse and cow;
There varnished straws were lying thick
  Paving with streaky gold the trodden silver snow.

Such light filled me with awe
  And nothing marred my paradisal thought,
That robin least of all I saw
  Lying too fast asleep, his song choked in his throat.

Andrew Young (1885-1971), from *Collected Poems*
(1936)

Requiem for a Robin

  Our mother let us deal with it ourselves.
  She swore she'd never have another cat.
  We chose a spot beneath the apple tree
  Directly underneath the branch he sat
  And carolled on. We thought he would approve.
  It's hard to say exactly how it felt
  To take a spade and dig our friend a grave.
  We smoothed his feathers down and then I knelt
  To place him in the ground. He looked so small
  Compared to when he overflowed with song.

I shuddered when I covered him with earth
And hoped his mate would not grieve for too long.
We sang no hymns, but knew he would be heard
Where lamb lies down with lion, cat with bird.

Sue Cowling (1943-),
from *What is a Kumquat?* (1991)

Chapter 3

'Piously did Cover them with Leaves'

In addition to *Who Killed Cock Robin?*, it was the robin that covered the dead bodies of the Children, or Babes, in the Wood. The robin has several other traditional links with death (Chapter 7) and watches anyone digging, including at the graveside, where it cocks a careful eye for worms. Its singing has been frequently recorded at burials. The covering of bodies with moss and/or leaves could have arisen because it collects these as its usual nesting materials. It is not difficult, therefore, to see how a tale of the robin covering dead bodies might arise, but it is an extraordinary and persistent legend. It has been dismissed by previous commentators as 'an ancient belief', although in fact this is the earliest known record of robins covering the dead:

> 'A Robbyn read breast, fynding the dead body of a Man or Woman, will couer the face of the same with Mosse. And as some holdes opinion, he wyll couer also the whole body.'
>
> Thomas Lupton, from *A Thousand Notable Things of Sundrie Sort* (1579, reprinted several times)

Lupton's book was a jumbled collection from 'Latin writers…and some old English written books, and some also not long since printed.' He got much of his material from medieval bestiaries or Pliny's *Natural History*, but this idea is not found there, nor anything similar about a different bird that could have been transferred to a robin. We must assume he took it from British folk-lore, as it is not found outside Britain, and, in British folklore is only in connection with the *Children in the Wood*. The first record of the *Children in the*

Wood story comes from Norwich in 1595 by Thomas Millington, from which the ballad is presumably derived. The earliest extant copy of the ballad, reproduced here, is from the late seventeenth century. Although the robins occupy only two lines, they have been the chief cause of its popularity:

The Children in the Wood: or the Norfolk Gentleman's
Last Will and Testament

Now ponder well, you parents dear,
    These words which I shall write;
A doleful story you shall hear,
    In time brought forth to light.
A gentleman of good account
    In Norfolk dwelt of late,
Who did in honour far surmount
    Most men of his estate.

Sore sick he was and like to die,
    No help his life could save;
His wife by him as sick did lie,
    And both possessed one grave.
No love between these two was lost,
    Each was to other kind;
In love they lived, in love they died,
    And left two babes behind:

The one a fine and pretty boy
    Not passing three years old,
The other a girl more young than he,
    And framed in beauty's mould.
The father left his little son,
    As plainly did appear,
When he to perfect age should come,
    Three hundred pounds a year;

And to his little daughter Jane
     Five hundred pounds in gold,
To be paid down on marriage-day,
     Which might not be controlled.
But if the children chanced to die
     Ere they to age should come,
Their uncle should possess their wealth;
     For so the will did run.

'Now, brother' said the dying man,
     'Look to my children dear;
Be good unto my boy and girl,
     No friends else have they here:
To God and you I recommend
     My children dear this day;
But little while be sure we have
     Within this world to stay.

'You must be father and mother both,
     And uncle all in one;
God knows what will become of them
     When I am dead and gone.'
With that bespake the mother dear;
     'O brother kind', quoth she,
'You are the man must bring our babes
     To wealth or misery!

'And if you keep them carefully,
     Then God will you reward;
But if you otherwise should deal,
     God will your deeds regard.'
With lips as cold as any stone
     They kissed their children small:
'God bless you both, my children dear!'
     With that the tears did fall.

These speeches then their brother spake
    To this sick couple there:
'The keeping of your little ones,
    Sweet sister do not fear;
God never prosper me nor mine,
    Nor aught else that I have,
If I do wrong your children dear
    When you are laid in grave!'

The parents being dead and gone,
    The children home he takes,
And brings them straight unto his house,
    Where much of them he makes.
He had not kept these pretty babes
    A twelvemonth and a day,
But for their wealth, he did devise
    To make them both away.

He bargained with two ruffians strong,
    Which were of furious mood,
That they should take these children young,
    And slay them in a wood.
He told his wife an artful tale:
    He would the children send
To be brought up in London town
    With one that was his friend.

Away then went those pretty babes,
    Rejoicing at that tide,
Rejoicing with a merry mind
    They should on cock-horse ride.
They prate and prattle pleasantly,
    As they ride on their way,
To those that should their butchers be
    And work their lives' decay:

So that the pretty speech they had
Made Murder's heart relent;
And they that undertook the deed
Full sore now did repent.
Yet one of them, more hard of heart,
Did vow to do his charge,
Because the wretch that hired him
Had paid him very large.

The other won't agree thereto,
So here they fall to strife;
With one another they did fight
About the children's life;
And he that was of mildest mood
Did slay the other there,
Within an unfrequented wood.-
The babes did quake for fear!

He took the children by the hand,
Tears standing in their eye,
And bade them straightway follow him,
And look they did not cry;
And two long miles he led them on,
While they for food complain:
'Stay here', quoth he; 'I'll bring you bread
When I come back again.'

Those pretty babes, with hand in hand,
Went wandering up and down;
But never more could see the man
Approaching from the town.
Their pretty lips with blackberries
Were all besmeared and dyed;
And when they saw the darksome night,
They sat them down and cried.

Thus wandered these poor innocents,
    Till death did end their grief;
In one another's arms they died,
    As wanting due relief:
No burial this pretty pair
    From any man receives
Till robin redbreast piously
    Did cover them with leaves.

And now the heavy wrath of God
    Upon their uncle fell;
Yea, fearful fiends did haunt his house,
    His conscience felt an hell:
His barns were fired, his goods consumed
    His lands were barren made,
His cattle died within the field,
    And nothing with him stayed.

And in a voyage to Portugal
    Two of his sons did die;
And, to conclude, himself was brought
    To want and misery:
He pawned and mortgaged all his land
    Ere seven years came about.
And now at last his wicked act
    Did by this means come out.

The fellow that did take in hand
    These children for to kill,
Was for a robbery judged to die,
    Such was God's blessed will:
Who did confess the very truth,
    As here hath been displayed:
The uncle having died in jail,
    Where he for debt was laid.

A woodcut of the Children in the Wood by Harrison Weir from an illustrated edition of Sarah Trimmer's *History of the Robins*, c. 1870

You that executors be made,
    And overseers eke,
Of children that be fatherless,
    And infants mild and meek,
Take you example by this thing,
    And yield to each his right,
Lest God with suchlike misery
    Your wicked minds requite.

There have been several suggestions as to what the poem originally alluded to, including the princes in the Tower or, possibly, a rather undistinguished play of 1601, *Two Lamentable Tragedies*, by Robert Yarrington, although here the borrowing is probably by the playwright. There is a strong local tradition, very much alive today, which ascribes the death to Wayland Wood (or sometimes 'Wailing Wood'), near Watton in Norfolk, and the uncle's house as Griston Hall, still standing nearby.

Many ballads were topical in origin; indeed, this gave them their main point. The most plausible idea, expressed by Canon Kent in his *Land of the Babes in the Wood*, is that it was made up by Protestants as a bit of propaganda after a genuine incident in the area. The Protestant Thomas de Grey was the owner of Griston Hall in the mid-1500s but died when his son, also Thomas, was seven. He left this son to be brought up by his brother Robert, a Catholic Recusant. The son had been sold in marriage in infancy but then died himself, aged eleven, when visiting his (Protestant) step-mother. When Robert the Recusant tried then to take the dowry that little Thomas's widow would inherit, the locals immediately accused Robert of killing the boy for the money.

Two other reasons why the story is likely to date from the late sixteenth century are: (1) the reference in the last verse to 'overseers' is presumably to overseers of the poor, created by an act of 1572; (2) the 'voyage to Portugal' is unlikely to be entirely fictitious. Drake's expedition to Portugal of 1589 was disastrous, with only one sixth of the forces that took part returning. Millington's printing of 1595 was probably the first. Lupton presumably took his robin story from a different source and the two tales may have been merged, though in the ballad the robin uses leaves, whereas Lupton's uses moss.

Throughout the eighteenth century, the ballad was frequently reprinted in chap-books, sometimes in prose accounts, with acknowledgement to 'the ancient song'.

Sometimes, the people are given names, and the connection with Norfolk was often lost.

Joseph Addison, in *The Spectator* 1711, regarded it as 'one of the darling songs of the common people' and in the chapter on the redbreast in his *British Zoology* (1776), Thomas Pennant alluded to it as 'a composition of a most beautiful and pathetic simplicity…'

An allusion by John Gay, best known for his satirical Beggar's Opera[25], is worth quoting here:

from *The Shepherd's Week*

> Then sad he sung the Children in the Wood:
> (Ah, barbarous uncle, stained with infant blood!)
> How blackberries they plucked in deserts wild,
> And fearless at the glittering falchions smiled;
> Their little corpse the robin redbreasts found,
> And strewed with pious bill the leaves around.
> (Ah, gentle birds! if this verse lasts so long,
> Your name shall live for ever in my song).

John Gay (1685-1732)

Curiously, in 1814, the tale was introduced into verses designed to instruct the young in multiplication tables:

---

[25] The music of *The Beggar's Opera* is a collection of folk tunes arranged by Samuel Peppusch. The tune for Polly's song 'Oh ponder well, be not severe…' was the tune most probably used for the Children in the Wood, starting as it does with similar words.

Four times eight are thirty-two
    Brave sailors, stout and tall.
Who lately with Lord Collingwood
    Faced many a cannon-ball.
And four times nine are thirty-six
    Poor redbreasts of the wood;
In winter, when 'tis frost and snow,
    They visit man for food.
In time of old, two comely babes
    In wood were left forlorn,
Their lovely cheeks with berries dyed,
    Their hands with brambles torn;
Their hearts were sore oppressed with woe,
    They uttered many a sigh,
And glistening tears of innocence
    Hung trembling in their eye;
Till nature spent, beneath a tree,
    Kind death their pain relieves,
And robin redbreast, sacred bird,
    Did cover them with leaves.
Four tens are forty wild-flowers sweet
    That grow in Dian's grove;
Four times eleven are forty-four
    Young ladies – all in love –

from *Figures in Rhymes; or Metrical Computations addressed to Northumbrians*, by 'H.R.',

printed for J. Bell, Newcastle-upon-Tyne (1814)

and so on, until twelve times twelve is reached with a mixture of history, geography and natural history.

A nursery-rhyme of the mid nineteenth century clearly uses the same story, but this time with strawberry leaves.

> My dear, do you know
> How a long time ago,
> Two poor children
> Whose names I don't know,
> Were stolen away
> On a fine summer's day,
> And left in a wood,
> As I've heard people say.

And when it was night
So sad was their plight,
The sun it went down
And the moon gave no light!
They sobbed and they sighed,
And they bitterly cried,
And the poor little things
They laid down and died.

And when they were dead,
The robins so red
Brought strawberry leaves,
And over them spread;
And all the day long,
They sang them this song, –
Poor babes in the wood!
Poor babes in the wood!
And don't you remember
The babes in the wood?

Cited by J.O. Halliwell,
Popular Rhymes and Nursery Tales (1849)

The story survives today in another form – the Christmas pantomime. However, such a sad tale is quite inappropriate and the babes are rescued alive by *Robin* Hood! This deft sleight of translation was anticipated well before it first appeared as a pantomime:

from *The Ballad*

When Mary sat to sing or read,
    All sport and play stood still –
Her words could lock a wagon-wheel,
    And stop the march to drill.

Meanwhile, the tragic tale she told
Of babies in the Wood
And gentle Redbreast, - or that bold
Cock Robin, Robin Hood.

Thomas Hood (1799-1845)

At the beginning of the seventeenth century, the robin's covering of dead bodies suddenly found its way into great poetry, with one significant addition – these were bodies of murdered men. Lupton's account of 25 years earlier has been credited as the source but it is much more likely to be a popular tale of chivalry, told about St. George of England and some other saints and national heroes, by Richard Johnson, published in 1596 under the title *The Most Famous History of the Seven Champions of Christendom*. He may well have based his story on traditional tales, though the murder connection may be Johnson's own addition, as, quite possibly, is the legend that St. George was born in Coventry. There is no evidence that the real St. George ever set foot in England. The book was repeatedly reprinted in the seventeenth century, in shortened form in the eighteenth and bowdlerized in the nineteenth, since when it has largely disappeared. The quotations are taken from an early seventeenth century edition in the British Museum.

It tells, in more than forty pages, the story of fair Sabra who, after walking 'without the walls of Coventry', met the noble Earl of Coventry. When seeing her beauty he 'was ravished therewith, and deemed her the excellentest creature that ever nature framed', but, alas, 'the dart of love had shot from her beauteous cheeks into his heart not true love but lust.' He declares his passion at a dance, to which she replied 'your suit and unlawful desire I do detest as much as the sight of a crocodile'.

The following morning, he approached her in an orchard with a poniard (a small dagger), threatening to ravish her by force and cut off her tongue and hands, at which Sabra fainted. On reviving, she pretended to fall in with his plans, provided that they could 'sit some certain hours upon this bed of violets and bewail the loss of my good name, which shortly shall be yielded up to your pleasure'. She tried to lull him to sleep with various tales, eventually succeeding, after invoking the god of sleep, the bees, the silver streams and the whispering winds, with a 'woeful ditty', including the words 'And let this sleep be thy Eternal Night'. She then picked up the dagger and sheathed it 'up to the tree in the closure of his breast' so that 'his soul was forced to give the world a doleful adieu'.

Observing the blood stains everywhere, including on her own clothing she 'ran speedily unto the flowing fountain, that stood on the further side of the orchard, and began to wash the blood out of her clothes, but the more she washed the more it increased', after which she 'tore her blood-stained garment from her back and cast it into the fountain':

> 'Thus being disrobed into her petticoat, she returned to the slaughtered Earl, whose face[26] she found covered with moss, which added more grief unto her sorrowful soul, for she greatly feared her murder was descried: but it fell not out as she mistrusted, for it is the nature and kind of robin redbreast, and other birds, always to cover the face of any dead man, and those were they that bred this fear in the lady's heart.'

This is the end of the robin incident[27] but, just to complete the story: Sabra was found and taken to the king who sent her to prison for twelve months, after which she was to be burned unless she could find a knight-at-arms to be her champion, and be victorious, during that time. After a year, a pyre was built, and the Baron of Chester summoned as the challenger. No champion appeared for an hour after which she pleaded 'Heaven show present vengeance upon me by fire, else some noble champion save my body alive'. At which point, people heard the horn of St. George, summoned back five months before from Egypt. He now arrived on a coal-black palfrey, fought

---

[26] 'body' in some editions
[27] The book contains several other references to animal lore, e.g. the swan's dying song and lions as a test for virginity.

the challenger, slew him and 'most courteously received [Sabra]'; and 'so great was the joy throughout the city that the bells rang without ceasing for three days together'.

In a second part of the *Seven Champions*, which appeared in 1597, there is another, rather similar, robin incident. Three of St. George's sons, on the borders of Lusitania (now parts of Portugal and Spain) found 'The Duke's daughter of Normandy tied by the locks of her own hair to the trunk of an orange tree', about to be ravished by three 'tawny-Moors'. The knights killed the Moors and unbound the girl, at which she said that her aged father, wrongfully deprived of his rights, was living in a hermitage nearby and that the Moors had bound him to a withered oak:

> 'When St. George's valiant sons (in company of this sorrowful maiden) came to the tree, they (contrary to their expectation) found her father cold and stiff, both devoid of sense and feeling, also finding his hands and face covered with green moss, which they supposed to be done by the robin redbreast and other little birds, who naturally cover the bare parts of any body that they find dead in the field, they fell into a new extremity of grief.'

The maiden determined to stay in the woods, while the sons of St. George departed.

The only other account of the legend, a compilation by Thomas Johnson, *Cornucopiae or Divers Secrets*, published in 1595 is clearly derived from Lupton's account.

All the poems that follow link the robin with death, and most concern the covering of dead bodies, though the first pre-dates any of these stories and the last few link it in other ways.

John Skelton wrote a mock mass for a Norwich schoolgirl's pet sparrow, killed by the local abbey cat. The first of its two parts stretches to no fewer than 833 lines, seen ostensibly through the girl's eyes, but demonstrating huge knowledge not just of birds but of history and liturgy, as well as exploring female sexuality. A short section follows:

from *A Lament for Philip Sparrow*

Lauda, anima mea, Dominum!

To weep with me, look that ye come,
All manner of birdes in your kind;
See none be left behind.
To mourning looke that ye fall
With dolorous songes funeral,
Some to sing, and some to say,
Some to weep, and some to pray,
Every birde in his lay.
The goldfinch, the wagtail;
The jangling jay to rail,
The flecked pie to chatter
Of this dolorous matter;
And robin redbreast,
He shall be the priest
The requiem mass to sing,
Softly warbeling,
With the help of the reed sparrow,
And the chatteringe swallow,
This hearse for to hallow;
The lark with his long toe;
The spink and the martinet also;
The shoveller with his broad beak;
The dotterel, that foolish peke,
And also the mad coot,
With balde face to boot,

(and it continues, mentioning many other birds)

John Skelton (?1460–1529)

The following five extracts were all written between 1595 and 1616, demonstrating the immediate and enormous popularity of the legend.

from *The Owle*

And every bird showed in his proper kind
What virtue nature had to him assigned.
The pretty turtle and the kissing dove,
Their faiths in wedlock, and chaste nuptial love:
The hens (to women) sanctity express,
Hallowing their eggs: the swallow's cleanliness
Sweeting her nest and purging it of dung,
And every hour is picking of her young.
The hern, by soaring shows tempestuous showers,
The princely cock distinguisheth the hours,
The kite, his train him guiding in the air,
Prescribes the helm, instructing how to steer.
The crane to labour, fearing some rough flaw,
With sand and gravel burdening his craw:
Noted by man, which by the same did find
To ballast ships for steadiness in wind.
And by the form and order in his flight,
To march in war, and how to watch by night.
The first of house that ere did groundsel lay,
Which then was homely, of rude loan and clay,
Learned of the martin: philomel in spring,
Teaching by art her little one to sing;
By whose clear voice sweet music first was found,
Before Amphion ever knew a sound.
Covering with moss the dead's unclosed eye,
The little redbreast teacheth charity.
So many there in sundry things excel,
Time scarce could serve their properties to tell.

Michael Drayton (1563-1631)

from *Euthymiae Raptus* or *The Tears of peace*

And then, did all the horrid wood appear,
Where mortal dangers, more than leaves did grow;
In which we could not one free step bestow
For treading on some murdered passenger
Who thither was by witchcraft forced to err:
Whose face the bird hid that loves humans best,
That hath the bugle eyes and rosy breast
And is the yellow autumn's nightingale.

George Chapman (?1559-1634)

from *Niobe Dissolved into a Nilus*

'Methinks I hear a melody that mocks the musician,
that pricks prick-song to the heart, and puts art to the
blush. O! 'tis the wretched Philomel; who, as Hesiodus
writeth, never sleepeth; but continually watcheth. And
when silence hath hushed the night into a dead sleep, she
then begins to carol out her care-tuned music, as if she
meant to ravish his mind that ravished her body. And, on
her, waits Robin, in his red livery, who sits as a crowner
on the murdered man, and seeing his body naked, plays
the sorry tailor, to make him a mossy raiment.'

Anthony Stafford (1587-1645)

Scene leading to *The Dirge for Imogen* (from *Cymbeline*)

Enter Arviragus bearing Imogen, disguised as Fidele, in his arms

Arviragus: With fairest flowers,
        Whilst summer lasts, and I live here, Fidele,
        I'll sweeten thy sad grave: thou shalt not lack
        The flower that's like thy face, pale primrose, nor
        The azured harebell, like thy veins; no, nor
        The leaf of eglantine, whom not to slander,
        Out-sweetened not thy breath: the Ruddock would
        With charitable[28] bill – O bill sore shaming
        Those rich-left heirs that let their fathers lie
        Without a monument! – bring thee all this;
        Yea, and furred moss besides, when flowers are none,
        To winter-ground thy corse.
Guiderius: Prithee have done;
        And do not play in wench-like words with that
        Which is so serious. Let us bury him,
        And not protract with admiration what
        Is now due debt. To the grave.
Arviragus: Say, where shall's lay him?
Guiderius: By good Euriphile, our mother.
Arviragus: Be't so:
        And let us, Polydore, though now our voices
        Have got the mannish crack, sing him to the ground,
        As once our mother; use like note and words,
        Save that 'Euriphile' must be 'Fidele'.

William Shakespeare (1564-1616)

---

[28] The reference to charity is a clear echo of Drayton's earlier poem quoted above.

The Dirge for Marcello (from *The White Devil*)

[Flamineo has murdered his brother, Marcello, and a friend mentions that he has heard their mother lamenting. The mother, Cornelia, then enters with Marcello's body, borne by three other ladies:]

Cornelia:	Will you make me such a fool? here's a white hand:
	Can blood so soon be washed out? let me see;
	When screech-owls croak upon the chimney-tops,
	And the strange cricket i' the oven sings and hops,
	When yellow spots do on your hands appear,
	Be certain then you of a corse shall hear.
	Out upon't, how 'tis speckled! h'as handled a toad, sure.
	Cowslip-water is good for the memory:
	Pray, buy me three ounces of't.
Flamineo:	I would I were from hence.
Cornelia:	Do you hear, sir?
	I'll give you a saying which my grandmother
	Was wont, when she heard the bell toll, to sing o'er
	Unto her lute.
Flamineo:	Do, an you will, do.
	(Cornelia doth this in several forms of distraction)
Cornelia:	'Call for the robin redbreast and the wren,
	Since o'er shady groves they hover,
	And with leaves and flowers do cover
	The friendless bodies of unburied men.
	Call unto his funeral dole
	The ant, the field-mouse, and the mole,
	To rear him hillocks that shall keep him warm,
	And (when gay tombs are robbed) sustain no harm:
	But keep the wolf far thence, that's foe to men,
	For with his nails he'll dig them up again.'
	They would not bury him 'cause he died in quarrel;
	But I have as answer for them:
	'Let holy church receive him duly,
	Since he paid the church-tithes truly.'

John Webster (?1580–?1625)

69

The theme was taken up again later in the seventeenth century. Robert Herrick had a particular fondness for the robin, at least partly because of its allusion to his own name. His *Upon Mrs Eliz: Wheeler* strikes a particularly charming note. One addition is that the robin is regarded as the 'sexton' of the woods, perhaps from one of the traditional versions of the tale. Following these, I have included some later references.

How Rubert the Robin spoke to the Eagle,
from *The Pleasant History of Cawwood the Rook*

[Rubert the Robin is stating his claim to be King of the Birds in the temporary absence of the eagle.]

My Lord the Eagle, I hope Rubert the Robin is not unknown to you, whom men women and children do love, honour and respect; no piece is discharged against me, no snare set for me, so that I fly with safety into houses, butteries and cellars, because no man will hurt a robin. The reason why I am beloved is for my courtesy and familiarity towards men, for if I find a dead body in the wood, I and the rest of my fellows do bury it with moss and leaves, and for this I am called the Sexton of the Wood: besides, I sing in winter, neither can the coldest frosts put me down, when all the other birds like cowards creep into bushes. I therefore having the better, and being generally beloved, do know no reason why I may not govern the Commonwealth of Birds in your royal absence.

The moral

It is some argument of worth in ourselves when we are beloved of others, as appears by the speech of Rubert the Robin, who urges it as a praise unto himself to be beloved of men.

Anonymous (1640)

To Robin Redbreast

Laid out for dead, let thy last kindness be
With leaves and moss-work for to cover me:
And while the wood-nymphs my cold corpse inter,
Sing thou my dirge, sweet-warbling chorister!
For epitaph, in foliage, next write this,
Here, here the Tomb of Robin Herrick is.

Robert Herrick (1591-1674)

To the Nightingale, and Robin Redbreast

When I departed am, ring thou my knell,
Thou pitiful, and pretty Philomel:
And when I'm laid out for a Corse, then be
Thou sexton (redbreast) for to cover me.

Robert Herrick

Upon Mrs Eliz: Wheeler, under the name of Amarillis

Sweet Amarillis, by a spring's
Soft and soul-melting murmurings,
Slept; and thus sleeping, thither flew
A robin redbreast, who at view,
Not seeing her at all to stir,
Brought leaves and moss to cover her:
But while he, perking, there did pry
About the arch of either eye,
The lid began to let out day,
At which poor robin flew away:
And seeing her not dead, but all disleaved;
He chirped for joy, to see himself deceived.

Robert Herrick

71

from *The Dead Sparrow*

Now this faithful bird is gone;
O let mournful turtles join
With loving red-breasts and combine
To sing dirges o'er his stone!

William Cartwright (1611–1643)

from *That a pleasant Poverty is to be preferred before discontented Riches*

Give me a river which doth scorn to show
    An added beauty; whose clear brow
    May be my looking-glass to see
What my face is, and what my mind should be!

Here waves call waves, and glide along in rank,
    And prattle to the smiling bank;
    Here sad kingfishers tell their tales,
And fish enrich the brook with silver scales.

Daisies, the first-born of the teeming spring,
　　On each side their embroidery bring;
　　Here lilies wash, and grow more white,
And daffodils, to see themselves, delight.

Here a fresh arbour gives her amorous shade,
　　Which Nature, the best gardener, made.
　　Here I would sit and sing rude lays,
Such as the nymphs and me myself should please.

Thus I would waste, thus end, my careless days;
　　And robin redbreasts, whom men praise
　　For pious birds, should, when I die,
Make both my monument and elegy.

Abraham Cowley (1618-1667)[29]

from *The Turtle and the Sparrow*

Sing Philomel his funeral verse,
Ye pious redbreast deck his hearse;
Fair swans extend your dying throats,
Columbo's death requires your notes.

Mathew Prior (1664-1721)

---

[29] The first three verses are omitted. His actual experiences, when he did retire to the country, were much less pleasant. 'The first night ... I caught so great a cold ... as made me keep to my chamber ten day. And, two after, had such a bruise on my ribs with a fall... And besides, I can get no money from my tenants, and have my meadows eaten up every night by cattle.' (Samuel Johnson *Lives of the Poets*, 1789)

A Song from Shakespeare's Cymbeline

To fair Fidele's grassy tomb
    Soft maids and village hinds shall bring
Each opening sweet, of earliest bloom,
    And rifle all the breathing spring.

No wailing ghost shall dare appear
    To vex with shrieks this quiet grove,
But shepherd lads assemble here,
    And melting virgins own their love.

No withered witch shall here be seen,
    No goblins lead their nightly crew;
The female fays shall haunt the green,
    And dress thy grave with pearly dew!

The redbreast oft at evening hours
    Shall kindly lend his little aid,
With hoary moss and gathered flowers,
    To deck the ground where thou art laid.

When howling winds and beating rain
    In tempests shake the sylvan cell;
Or 'midst the chase on every plain
    The tender thought on thee shall dwell.

Each lonely scene shall thee restore,
    For thee the tear be duly shed;
Beloved till life could charm no more;
    And mourned till Pity's self be dead.

William Collins (1721-1759)

The final group associate robins with death in other ways:

A Woodland Murder

He murdered her alone at dead midnight
While the pale moon threw round her sickly light
Loud screams assailed the thicket's slumbers deep
But only scared the little birds from sleep
When the pale murderer's terror-frowning eye
Told its dread errand – that the maid should die
Mid thick blackthorns her secret grave was made
And there the unresisting corpse was laid
When no one saw the deed but God and he
And moonlight sparkling through the sleeping tree
The robin redbreast might at morning steal
There, for the worm to meet his early meal
In fresh-turned moulds which first beheld the sun –
Nor know the deed that dismal night had done

John Clare (1793-1864), from *The Shepherd's Calendar*

Proud Maisie

Proud Maisie is in the wood,
        Walking so early;
Sweet Robin sits on the bush,
        Singing so rarely.

'Tell me, thou bonny bird,
        When shall I marry me?'
'When six braw gentlemen
        Kirkward shall carry ye.'

'Who makes the bridal bed,
       Birdie, say truly?'
'The grey-headed sexton
       That delves the grave duly.

'The glow-worm o'er grave and stone
       Shall light thee steady;
The owl from the steeple sing
       'Welcome, proud lady!"

Sir Walter Scott (1771-1832)

A Simple Funeral

'Some time since, the funeral of an aged and most respected lady took place in the beautiful neighbourhood of Dunster. Amongst the 'followers' was a robin, who took an active part in the ceremonies by singing during the entire service. His seat was on a spray close by the grave. The old lady had expressed a wish to be buried in autumn; and it is a touching coincidence that her *requiem* should have been chanted by autumn's sole chorister. Let me add – the clergyman who officiated was much affected by this accompaniment of the church's rites.'

'Philocyon' (Braintree) in *Kidd's Own Journal* (1853)[30]

Inevitably, this chapter has been mainly sombre in tone, so I will finish on a light note. A robin sang for Miss Ellen Gee of Kew, who died when stung in the eye by a bee. The verse was published anonymously but bears the hallmark of Horace Smith:

---

[30] William Kidd of Hammersmith published his journal only from 1852-54. He was described by H.G. Adams, in *Our Feathered Families*, 1862, as 'that most genial and bird-like of men, whose soul overflows with love and humanity'. His favoured subjects were kindness of heart, feminine fashions and robins. (see also Chapters 8 and 9)

Ye nymphs of Q, then shun each B,
 List to the reason Y;
For should A B C U at T,
 He'll surely sting your I,
Now in a grave L deep in Q,
 She's cold as cold can B;
Whilst robins sing upon A U
 Her dirge and L E G.

      ?Horatio (Horace) Smith (1779-1849)

*A woodcut from the Roxburghe Ballads edition of 1595, the earliest
depiction of robins covering the Children in the Wood.*

Chapter 4
Robins and Prisoners

In the year 1637, Dr. John Bastwick, with William Prynne who recorded the events, was tried before the court of the Star Chamber on account of his violent denunciation of the bishops. He was sentenced to a fine of £5,000, the pillory, loss of his ears, and imprisonment for life. At the pillory he graciously thanked everyone before having his ears cut off. With undoubted courage, he uttered pieties about God counting him worthy, and that he was maintaining the 'truth of God, and the honour of my king against popish usurpations.' He was imprisoned in Launceston Castle, but then:

> 'the High Sheriff of Cornwall caused Doctor Bastwick to be suddenly removed without any warning from Launceston to Plymouth, upon the 10th day of October, 1637, where being embarked in a small vessel (into which his wife was not permitted to enter, to take her farewell of him) he landed at the Islands of Scillies the 16th of the same October, where many thousands of robin redbreasts (none of which birds were ever seen in those Islands before or since) newly arrived at the castle there the evening before, welcomed him with their melody, and within one day or two after took their flight from thence, no man knows whither.[31]'

William Prynne, in *A New Discovery of the Prelates' Tyranny* (1641)

[Bastwick was eventually released by the Long Parliament.]

---

[31] The Rev. C. Swainson quoted this incident in *The Folklore and Provincial Names of British Birds* (1886), adding 'These birds were evidently regarded as a sign of the captive's future deliverance'. However, there is no evidence from the original source that Bastwick saw it this way. He was only released three years later.

At the present time, the robin breeds on the Isles of Scilly, but it may not have done so in the seventeenth century, and in either case, so large a number in October suggests a passage of migrants. (Chapter 9)

The robin already had a reputation of cheering up prisoners. This extract refers also to the Babes in the Wood legend (see Chapter 3).

To cheer up a Prisoner

'A small end of a cord saves a man from drowning, and a finger of a friend to a prisoner is a full hand.

'They that cheer up a prisoner but with their sight are robin redbreasts, that bring straws in their bills to cover a dead man in extremity; such acquaintances grow like strawberries in a barren country: you shall hardly in a day gather a handful.

'Account those therefore in whose society thy purse hath been ever open, and whose hands are shut to thee in prison, but as dunghills on which the sun hath shined: for his golden beams, they pay stinking and unsavoury smells.'

Thomas Dekker (1570?-1641?), in *Villainies discovered by Lanthorne and Candle-light* (1616)

Another robin visited the cell window of James Montgomery each day, when he was briefly imprisoned for a minor offence in York Castle, in February, 1795:

from *Verses to a Robin Redbreast*

Welcome! pretty little stranger!
Welcome to my lone retreat!

79

Here, secure from every danger,
Hop about and chirp and eat.
Robin! How I envy thee,
Happy child of Liberty!

Now, though tyrant Winter howling,
Shakes the world with tempests round:
Heaven above with vapours scowling,
Frost imprisons all the ground;
Robin! what are these to thee?
Thou art blessed with liberty.

James Montgomery

In this vein, the poet continued for five more similar, and fairly tedious, verses, but they were popular at the time.

Birds have nearly always been associated with comforting prisoners, but the robin has been credited with an opposite effect in Germany, where:

> 'so sad is its song that prisoners have died from grief within their dungeons from hearing the thrilling sensations of loneliness conveyed in the song of the redbreast.'

J.J. Watters, from *The Natural History of the Birds of Ireland* (1883)

Four hundred years earlier, a robin, among other birds, embodied the idea of liberty to a poet who was not a captive in the conventional sense but a Benedictine monk (and a friend of Chaucer's son), evidently feeling the constraints of monastic life:

from *The Flour of Curtesye*

And whyle that I, in my drery payne,
Sate and behelde aboute on every tre
The foules sytte, always twayne and twayne,
Than thought I thus: 'alas! what may this be,
That every foule hath his lyberte
Frely to chose after his desyre
Everyche his make thus, fro yere to yere?

The sely wrenne, the tytemose also,
The lytel redbrest, have free election
To flyen yfere and togyther go
Where as hem lyst, aboute envyron,
As they of kynde have inclynacion,
And as Nature, emperesse and gyde,
Of every thyng, lyste to provyde;

81

But man alone, alas, the harde stounde,
Ful cruelly, by kyndes ordynaunce,
Constrayned is, and by statute bounde,
And debarred from al suche plesaunce.
What meneth this? What is this purveyaunce
Of God above, agayne al right of kynde,
Withoute cause, so narowe man to bynde?'

John Lydgate (1370–1449)

Wordsworth, in the 'captivity' of old age, could be comforted by the memory of a robin:

I know an aged Man constrained to dwell
In a large house of public charity,
Where he abides, as in a Prisoner's cell,
With numbers near, alas! no company.

When he could creep about, at will, though poor
And forced to live on alms, this old Man fed
A Redbreast, one that to his cottage door
Came not, but in a lane partook his bread.

There at the root of one particular tree,
An easy seat this worn-out Labourer found
While Robin pecked the crumbs upon his knee
Laid one by one, or scattered on the ground.

Dear intercourse was theirs, day after day;
What signs of mutual gladness when they met!
Think of their common peace, their simple play,
The parting moment and its fond regret.

Months passed in love that failed not to fulfil,
In spite of season's change, its own demand,
By fluttering pinions here and busy bill;
There by caresses from a tremulous hand,

82

Thus in the chosen spot a tie so strong
Was formed between the solitary pair,
That when his fate had housed him 'mid a throng
The Captive shunned all converse proffered there.

Wife, children, kindred, they were dead and gone;
But, if no evil hap his wishes crossed,
One living Stay was left, and on that one
Some recompense for all that he had lost.

O that the good old Man had power to prove,
By message sent through air or visible token,
That he still loves the Bird, and still must love;
That friendship lasts though fellowship is broken!

William Wordsworth (c. 1846)

In view of the robin's literary associations with death, it is pleasing to find two cases in which the bird has been linked with the execution of an English criminal. In Chester, on 6 April 1796, James Price and Thomas Brown were 'charged on oath, with a strong suspicion of having …feloniously assaulted Peter Yoxall, who was carrying on horseback His Majesty's mail, from Warrington in the county of Lancaster to the city of Chester, and taking from his person the said mail bag with the letters and other articles contained therein' (from a statement about the trial by E. Monk, Chester, 1796). The accused confessed to the crime, and were hanged in chains at Trafford Green. The place was enclosed, and the bodies remained there until the pole was taken down in 1820, when it was discovered that a robin had built its nest in Price's skull. This occasioned the following rhyme:

Oh! James Price deserved his fate:
Naught but robbing in his pate
Whilst alive, and now he's dead
Has still robin in his head.

High he swings for robbing the mail
But his brain of robin female
Still is quite full; though out of breath
The passion e'en survives his death.

Egerton Leigh, *Ballads and Legends of Cheshire* (1867)

A more dramatic incident occurred in 1833, a time of poverty and unrest in the English countryside. George Wren, a Sussex boy aged nineteen, was accused of setting fire to a haystack. The main evidence was the discovery of footprints which fitted his boots, these being found on the side of the stack away from that on which Wren and others later tried to put out the fire. Many people thought the boy innocent, but the jury, influenced by the judge's unfavourable summing-up, brought in a verdict of guilty, though with a strong recommendation for mercy. The judge ignored the recommendation, and sentenced the prisoner to death. The following is an extract from the front page of the Brighton Herald, for 12 January 1833:

EXECUTION OF GEORGE WREN FOR ARSON

'This ill-fated young man, who was only 19 years of age, expiated his crime on Saturday morning last, on the scaffold, in front of Horsham Gaol. From the time of his condemnation at Lewes …the convict had conducted himself with the greatest levity, obstinately denying his guilt in the transaction for which he was about to suffer. The night previous to his execution he retired early to rest, and slept soundly the whole night, until awakened by the turnkey at 7 in the morning, when he said he should have slept two hours longer if he had not been called… He manifestly appeared to retain a strong feeling of resentment against many persons in the neighbourhood in which he resided, and so strong did that feeling appear, and as no exhortation on the part of the Chaplain, nor others by whom he was visited, could diminish it, or persuade him to die in Christian charity with all, the Rev. gentleman declined to request him to partake of the Holy Sacrament … Being asked if he had anything to say, he immediately made a step forward, and resting upon one leg as far as the rope would allow him to get … he then addressed the populace for about ten minutes. The substance of his address, as far as we could gather, was this:

' "Good people – I am brought to this fatal scaffold to be murdered! – to be murdered, I say, for a thing I know nothing of … If it should fall to any of your lot, good people, any of you who may be likely to be suspected like me who stands here before you, if you see a fire don't go near it – not that I should like to see the country burn – but by going to this fire, and fetching water, and I tried every measure to put out the fire, but by the track of my shoe in fetching water, I was found guilty. I was condemned by the people of Uckfield, but God forbid I should accuse all the people of that parish." … "I die innocent, so help me God! Fare you well all."

'He then drew himself back under the beam, and the crowd immediately began to disperse.'

On an inner page of the same issue of the Brighton Herald appeared the following:

'GEORGE WREN –It is particularly stated in Horsham and the neighbourhood, that, on Saturday last, while the body of Wren was hanging the usual hour, a robin settled upon his feet, and being disturbed, flew to a short distance and then returned to its former position. The circumstance is considered by the country people as ominous of the innocence of the deceased.'

(a full account is quoted by William Alberry in
A Millennium of Facts in the History of Horsham and Sussex,
947-1947 (Horsham Museum Society, 1947)

This grim 'Robin and Wren' story has a sequel. A few years later at Brighton, a man confessed on his death-bed that he had fired the haystack in question, and had used Wren's boots while doing so. Poor Wren's 'levity' in protesting his innocence was, after all, justified.

Robin the mail

Chapter 5

'Robin Redbreast tunes his Note'

'There is a little bird rather celebrated for its affection to mankind than its singing, which, however, in our climate has the sweetest note of all others. The note of other birds is louder, and their inflexions more capricious, but this bird's voice is soft, tender and well supported, and the more to be valued as we enjoy it the greatest part of the winter.'

Oliver Goldsmith (1728-1774), from *A History of the Earth and Animated Nature* (1774)

The song of the robin has been celebrated across the centuries by many of our greatest poets. One of the main reasons is that the robin sings almost throughout the year, and so evokes many different moods[32]. Thus, selection of poems can be more diverse than for most other birds.

from *The Birds of Scotland*

Each season in its turn he hails; he hails,
Perched on the naked tree, spring's earliest bud:
At morn, at chilly eve, when the March sun
Sinks with a wintry tinge, and Hesper sheds
A frosty light, he ceases not his sheds

---

[32] The wren is perhaps the only other bird that sings all year round. This may be one reason for its association with the robin. The wren's song always seems optimistic and, however welcome it is, it does not evoke such a range of emotion as that of the robin.

And when staid Autumn walks with rustling tread,
He mourns the falling leaf. E'en when each branch
Is leafless, and the harvest morn has clothed
The fields in white, he, on the hoar-plumed spray,
Delights, dear trustful bird!

James Grahame (1765-1811)

In Britain, young robins can start to sing in late July, the adults following some time in August, once they have finished their midsummer moult. They will sing through to November. After this, their song becomes more subdued during the rains of early winter and during cold weather. The louder spring song can be heard from late December on bright or warm days, offering a promise of spring months. Later, when the leaves and flowers have appeared, the robin is only one of many, and its modest contribution is almost obscured, though never forgotten:

> 'It is the opinion of some, that this little King of Birds, for sweetness of Note comes not much short of the nightingale.'

Nicholas Cox, from The Gentleman's Recreation
(c.1676)[33]

By contrast, one of our greatest naturalists, Gilbert White, whose writings one might expect to see well represented in this book, appears to have disliked robins:

> '16th October 1776: The redbreast's note is very sweet and pleasing; did it not carry with it ugly associations of ideas, and put us in mind of the approach of winter.'

Gilbert White (1720-1793), from Gilbert White's Journals,
ed W. Johnson (1931)[34]

---

[33] This book is noteworthy for bringing the 'red herring' into the language, a red or smoked herring (i.e., a kipper), having a strong smell and recommended as a distraction for hounds during the hunt.

[34] For White's other, even more negative, opinions on robins, see p. 206

I have placed the poems in chronological order of poets throughout this chapter, and the next. In so doing, we see a progression through the seasons of the year, although there are exceptions. The earliest extract, from 1400, and those from Elizabethan times extol the spring, usually the month of May. For the Elizabethans, the nightingale was the supreme songster, coming with the classical poetic tradition from the Mediterranean. It fitted the Elizabethan mood of hopeless passion, and it is the glory of May. The robin is mainly mentioned in passing, as befits its role in the spring chorus.

There follows a striking gap in robin poems generally between about 1660 and 1760, almost the only exceptions being James Thomson's *The Seasons*, quoted in Chapter 1 and the political 'Robins' in Chapter 8. Then in the latter part of the eighteenth century, the robin came into its own. Autumnal melancholy, or at least wistfulness, fitted the mood of the Romantics and with the autumn, came the robins. The robin provides the most characteristic music of the countryside in autumn, to the envy of the Continent. Outside Britain at this season, the robin sings rather feebly and spasmodically.

It may seem surprising to us that the beauties of the English autumn were for so long unrecognised, or unsung. But in harder times, the approach of winter was something to dread rather than welcome. Later, a well-stocked larder and the rise in domestic comfort probably had an important influence. It is significant that 'wild', or unproductive, scenery became popular at the same time. There was an outburst of poetry in the pastoral style, pre-eminent among them being our two best known naturalist-poets, William Wordsworth and John Clare.

This period sees robins featuring in some of our greatest poetry, surrounded, inevitably, by other poems that are placid and dull. Yet even these evoke an atmosphere of rural contentment - somewhat misleadingly, as they ignore the poverty of the labourer and the gathering smoke palls of the towns and cities where men - and sometimes robins - were living stunted lives. The many poorer poems on the robin's song, and passing tributes in poems of a more general nature have been omitted, including many of those in *The Robin's Jubilee* of 1826.

from *The Tale of Beryn*

Who sawe evir so feir or so glad a day?
And how sote this seson is, entring in to May.
The thrustelis and the thrusshis in this glad mornyng,
The ruddok and the goldfynch; but the nyghtyngale,
His amerous notis, lo, how he twynyth smale!
Lo! how the trees grenyth, that nakid wer and nothing bare
This month afore; but now hir somer clothing wear.
Lo! how nature makith for hem everichone!
And, as many as ther been, he forgetith noon!
Lo! howe the seson of the yer, and Averell shouris,
Doith the busshis burgyn out blosomis, and flouris!
Lo! the pryme-rosis, how fressh they been to seen!
And many othir flouris a-mong the grasis grene,
Lo! howe they spryng, and sprede, and of divers hewe!
Be-holdith and seith both rede, white, and blewe,
That lusty been, and confortabill for mannys sighte!
For I sey, for my selff, It makith my hert to lighte!

Anonymous (c. 1400)

Epithalamion

    Wake now, my love, awake! For it is time;
    The rosy morn long since left Tithon's bed,
    All ready to her silver coach to climb;
    And Phoebus 'gins to show his glorious head.
    Hark! how the cheerful birds do chant their lays,
    And carol of love's praise.
    The merry lark her matins sings aloft;
    The thrush replies; the mavis descant plays;
    The ouzel shrills; the ruddock warbles soft;

So goodly all agree with sweet consent
To this day's merriment.
Ah! my dear love, why do ye sleep this long,
When meeter were that ye should now awake,
T'await the coming of your joyous make,
And hearken to the birds' love-learned song,
The dewy leaves among?
For they of joy and pleasance to you sing,
That all the woods them answer, and their echo ring.

Edmund Spenser
(1552? – 99)

Spring's Welcome

WHAT bird so sings, yet so does wail?
O 'tis the ravish'd nightingale.
Jug, jug, jug, jug, tereu! she cries,
And still her woes at midnight rise.
Brave prick-song! Who is't now we hear?
None but the lark so shrill and clear;
Now at heaven's gate she claps her wings,
The morn not waking till she sings.
Hark, hark, with what a pretty throat
Poor robin redbreast tunes his note!
Hark how the jolly cuckoos sing
Cuckoo! to welcome in the spring!
Cuckoo! to welcome in the spring!

John Lyly (1553–1606)

Illustration from Lady Lindsay's *About Robins* (1889)

Song from *The Rape of Lucrece*

Pack, clouds, away! And welcome, day!
  With night we banish sorrow.
Sweet air, blow soft; mount, lark, aloft
  To give my Love good-morrow!
Wings from the wind to please her mind,
  Notes from the lark I'll borrow:
Bird, prune thy wing, nightingale, sing!
  To give my Love good-morrow!
  To give my Love good-morrow
  Notes from them all I'll borrow.

Wake from thy nest, robin redbreast!
  Sing, birds in every furrow!
And from each hill let music shrill
  Give my fair Love good-morrow!
Black bird and thrush in every bush,
  Stare, linnet and cocksparrow,
You pretty elves, among yourselves
  Sing my fair Love good-morrow!
  To give my Love good-morrow
  Sing, birds, in every furrow!

                    Thomas Heywood (157?–1650)

An Epithalamion (or Marriage Song)

*On Frederick, Count Palatine of the Rhine, and
Lady Elizabeth, being married of St. Valentine's Day*

Hail Bishop Valentine! whose day this is,
  All the air is thy diocese,

And all the chirping choristers
And other birds are thy parishioners:
  Thou marriest every year
The lyric lark, and the grave whispering dove;
The sparrow, that neglects his life for love;
The household bird, with the red stomacher;
  Thou mak'st the blackbird speed as soon
As doth the goldfinch, or the halcyon;
The husband cock looks out and straight is sped,
And meets his wife, which brings her feather-bed.
This day more cheerfully than ever shine;
This day, which might enflame thyself, Old Valentine! ...

John Donne (1573 – 1631)

from *The Affectionate Shepherd*[35]

And when th'art weary of thy keeping sheep
Upon a lovely down, to please thy mind
I'll give thee fine ruff-footed doves to keep,
And pretty pigeons of another kind:
A robin-redbreast shall thy minstrel be,
Chirping thee sweet and pleasant melody.

Richard Barnfield (1574-1620)

---

[35] This long poem is full of homo-erotic imagery, the robin here thought to symbolise a penis, as it is in folklore from some parts of the country. Other birds are mentioned straight after this but all in context of how to catch them for the pot.

from Britannia's Pastorals

The lily-handed morn
Saw Phoebus stealing dew from Ceres' corn.
The mounting lark (day's herald) got on wing,
Bidding each bird choose out his bough and sing.
The lofty treble sang the little wren;
Robin the mean, that best of all loves men;
The nightingale the tenor, and the thrush
The counter-tenor sweetly in a bush.
And that the music might be full in parts,
Birds from the grove flew with right willing hearts;

William Browne (1591–1645)

To Phillis, to love and live with him

Live, live with me, and thou shalt see
The pleasures I'll prepare for thee:
What sweets the country can afford
Shall bless thy bed, and bless thy board.
The soft sweet moss shall be thy bed,
With crawling woodbine over-spread:
By which the silver-shredding streams
Shall gently melt thee into dreams.
Thy clothing next, shall be a gown
Made of the fleece's purest down.
The tongues of kids shall be thy meat;
Their milk thy drink; and thou shalt eat
The paste of filberts for thy bread
With cream of cowslips butterèd:
Thy feasting-tables shall be hills
With daisies spread, and daffodils;
Where thou shalt sit, and redbreast by,

For meat, shall give thee melody.
I'll give thee chains and carcanets
Of primroses and violets.
A bag and bottle thou shalt have;
That richly wrought, and this as brave;
So that as either shall express
The wearer's no mean shepherdess.

Robert Herrick (1591–1674)

Ode

Poor bird! I do not envy thee;
Pleased in the gentle melody
  Of thy own song.
Let crabbed winter silence all
The winged choir; he never shall
  Chain up thy tongue:
    Poor innocent!
When I would please myself, I look on thee,
And guess some sparks of that felicity,
  That self-content.

When the bleak face of winter spreads
The earth, and violates the meads
  Of all their pride;
When sapless trees and flowers are fled,
Back to their causes, and lie dead
  To all beside:
    I see thee set,
Bidding defiance to the bitter air,
Upon a withered spray; by cold made bare,
  And drooping yet.

There, full in notes, to ravish all
My earth, I wonder what to call
  My dullness; when

I hear thee, pretty creature, bring
Thy better odes of praise, and sing,
  To puzzle men:
   Poor pious Elf!
I am instructed by thy harmony,
To sing the time's uncertainty,
  Safe in myself.

Poor redbreast, carol out thy lay,
And teach us mortals what to say.
  Here cease the choir
Of airy choristers; no more
Mingle your notes; but catch a store
  From her sweet lyre;
   You are but weak,
Mere summer chanters; you have neither wing
Nor voice, in winter. Pretty redbreast, sing,
  What I would speak.

George Daniel (1616–57)[36]

The Winter Walk at Noon

No noise is here, or none that hinders thought.
The redbreast warbles still, but is content
With slender notes and more than half suppressed:
Pleased with his solitude, and flitting light
From spray to spray, where'er he rests he shakes
From many a twig the pendent drops of ice,
That tinkle in the withered leaves below.
Stillness, accompanied with sounds so soft,
Charms more than silence. Meditation here
May think down hours to moments. Here the heart
May give a useful lesson to the head,

---

[36] Daniel described himself, with unnecessary harshness, as: 'all dullness. I was shaped only to flutter, in the lower Shrubbs of Earthborn follies'! This actually anticipates other poems on winter singing.

And learning wiser grow without his books.
Knowledge and wisdom, far from being one,
Have oft-times no connexion: knowledge dwells
In heads replete with thoughts of other men:
Wisdom in minds attentive to their own,
Knowledge, a rude unprofitable mass,
The mere materials with which wisdom builds,
Till smoothed and squared and fitted to its place,
Does but incumber whom it seems to enrich.
Knowledge is proud that he has learned so much;
Wisdom is humble that he knows no more.

William Cowper (1731–1800) from *The Task*

from *Ode to a Robin Redbreast*

Gentle bird a moment stay
Nor so soon amid the throng
Of feather'd folk the woods among,
Sweetly sing or wildly stray;
Gentle bird a moment stay—
Harmoniously a while to cheer
The sorrows of the drooping year,
Hoary winter to beguile,
And stretch his frost-fix'd features to a smile;
Gentle Robin stay a while!
With thy sweet thy artless lay,
Still hail the slowly-rising day;
And if Ceres' gifts can charm,
Or gratitude thy bosom warm,
Still to claim thy wonted meed,
At my window still to feed,
Still within my sight to play
Gentle bird a moment stay:

Hester Thrale (1741-1821)

from *The Humble Petition of Bruar Water to the Noble Duke of Athole*

> The sober laverock, warbling wild,
>   Shall to the skies aspire;
> The gowdspink, music's gayest child,
>   Shall sweetly join the choir:
> The blackbird stron, the lintwhite clear,
>   The mavis mild and mellow;
> The robin pensive autumn cheer
>   In all her locks of yellow.

Robert Burns (1759-96)

The Trossachs

There's not a nook within this solemn Pass,
But were an apt confessional for One
Taught by his summer spent, his autumn gone,
That Life is but a tale of morning grass
Withered at eve. From scenes of art which chase
That thought away, turn, and with watchful eyes
Feed it 'mid Nature's old felicities,
Rocks, rivers, and smooth lakes more clear than glass
Untouched, unbreathed upon. Thrice happy quest,
If from a golden perch of aspen spray
(October's workmanship to rival May)
The pensive warbler of the ruddy breast
That moral sweeten by a heaven-taught lay,
Lulling the year, with all its cares, to rest!

William Wordsworth (1770-1850)

from *Lines, written in the album of the Countess of Lonsdale*

Mute offerings, tribute from an inward sense
Of admiration and respectful love,
Have waited – till the affections could no more
Endure that silence, and broke out in song,
Snatches of music taken up and dropped
Like those self-solacing, those under, notes
Trilled by the redbreast, when autumnal leaves
Are thin upon the bough. Mine, only mine,
The pleasure was, and no one heard the praise,
Checked, in the moment of its issue, checked
And reprehended, by a fancied blush
From the pure qualities that called it forth.

William Wordsworth

from *The Prelude*

After the hour of sunset yester-even,
Sitting within doors between light and dark,
A choir of redbreasts gathered somewhere near
My threshold, - minstrels from the distant woods
Sent in on winter's service, to announce,
With preparation artful and benign
That the rough lord had left the surly North
On his accustomed journey. The delight,
Due to this timely notice, unawares
Smote me, and, listening, I in whispers said,
'Ye heartsome Choristers, ye and I will be
Associates, and, unscared by blustering winds,
Will chant together.'

William Wordsworth

from *To My Sister*

It is the first mild day of March:
Each minute sweeter than before,
The redbreast sings from the tall larch
That stands beside our door.

There is a blessing in the air,
Which seems a sense of joy to yield
To the bare trees, and mountains bare,
And grass in the green field.

William Wordsworth

from *September 1819*

Departing summer hath assumed
An aspect tenderly illumed,
The gentlest look of spring;
That calls from yonder leafy shade
Unfaded, yet prepared to fade,
A timely carolling.

No faint and hesitating trill,
Such tribute as to winter chill
The lonely redbreast pays!
Clear, loud, and lively is the din,
From social warblers gathering in
Their harvest of sweet lays.

William Wordsworth

To a Redbreast (In Sickness)

Stay, little cheerful Robin! stay,
    And at my casement sing.
Though it should prove a farewell lay
    And this our parting spring.

Though I, alas! may ne'er enjoy
    The promise in thy song;
A charm, that thought cannot destroy,
    Doth to thy strain belong.

Methinks that in my dying hour
    Thy song would still be dear,
And with a more than earthly power
    My passing spirit cheer.

Then, little bird, this boon confer,
    Come and my requiem sing,
Nor fail to be the harbinger
    Of everlasting spring.

Sara Hutchinson (c.1835)[37]

Frost at Midnight

So shalt thou see and hear
The lovely shapes and sounds intelligible
Of that eternal language, which thy God
Utters, who from eternity doth teach
Himself in all, and all things in himself.
Great universal Teacher! He shall mould
Thy spirit, and by giving make it ask.

---

[37] This poem is often printed in collections of Wordsworth's poems. She was his sister-in-law and Coleridge became infatuated with her.

Therefore all seasons shall be sweet to thee,
Whether the summer clothe the general earth
With greenness, or the redbreast sit and sing
Betwixt the tufts of snow on the bare branch
Of mossy apple-tree, while the nigh thatch
Smokes in the sun-thaw; whether the eave-drops fall
Heard only in the trances of the blast,
Or if the secret ministry of frost
Shall hang them up in silent icicles,
Quietly shining to the quiet moon.

Samuel Taylor Coleridge (1772-1834)

To the Robin

Sweet bard of autumn, silent is the song
Of earth and sky, that in the summer hour
Rang joyously, and thou alone art left
Sole minstrel of the dull and sinking year.
But trust me, warbler, lovelier lay than this,
Which now thou pourest to the chilling eve,
The joy-inspiring summer never knew.
The very children love to hear thy tale,
And talk of thee in many a legend wild,
And bless thee for those touching notes of thine!
Sweet household bird! that infancy and age
Delight to cherish, thou dost well repay
The frequent crumbs that generous hands bestow;
Beguiling man with minstrelsy divine,
And cheering his dark hours, and teaching him
Through cold and gloom, autumn and winter, Hope.

Noel Thomas Carrington (1777-1830)

Twenty-first Sunday after Trinity

The vision is yet for an appointed time, but at the end it shall speak and not lie; though it tarry, wait for it; because it will surely come, it will not tarry. —*Habakkuk, ii. 3.*

The Redbreast in September
25 September 1823

The morning mist is cleared away,
    Yet still the face of Heaven is grey,
Nor yet the autumnal breeze has stirred the grove,
    Faded yet full, a paler green
    Skirts soberly the tranquil scene,
The redbreast warbles round this leafy cove.

Sweet messenger of calm decay,
    Saluting sorrow as you may,
As one still bent to find or make the best,
    In thee, and in this quiet mead,
    The lesson of sweet peace I read,
Rather in all to be resigned than blest.

'Tis a low chant, according well
    With the soft solitary knell,
As homeward from some grave beloved we turn,
    Or by some holy death-bed dear,
    Most welcome to the chastened ear
Of her whom Heaven is teaching how to mourn.

O cheerful tender strain! The heart
    That duly bears with you its part,
Singing so thankful to the dreary blast,
    Though gone and spent its joyous prime,
    And on the world's autumnal time,
Mid withered hues and sere, its lot be cast:

That is the heart for thoughtful seer,
　　Watching, in trance nor dark nor clear,
The appalling Future as it nearer draws:
　　His spirit calmed the storm to meet,
　　Feeling the rock beneath his feet,
And tracing through the cloud the eternal Cause.

That is the heart for watchmen true
　　Waiting to see what God will do,
As o'er the church the gathering twilight falls:
　　No more he strains his wistful eye,
　　If chance the golden hours be nigh,
By youthful Hope seen beaming round her walls.

Forced from his shadowy paradise,
　　His thoughts to Heaven the steadier rise:
There seek his answer when the world reproves:
　　Contented in his darkling round,
　　If only he be faithful found
When from the east the eternal morning moves.

John Keble (1792-1866) in *The Christian Year* (1827)

Home Pictures in May

The sunshine bathes in clouds of many hues
And mornings feet are gemmed with early dews
Warm Daffodils about the garden beds
Peep thro their pale slim leaves their golden heads
Sweet earthly suns of spring – the Gosling broods
In coats of sunny green about the road
Waddle in extacy – and in rich moods
The old hen leads her flickering chicks abroad

Oft scuttling neath her wings to see the kite
Hang waving oer them in the springs blue light
The sparrows round their new nests chirp with glee
And sweet the Robin springs young luxury shares
Tuteling its song in feathery Goosberry tree
While watching worms the Gardeners spade unbears

John Clare (1793-1864)

from *The Eternity of Nature*

The little Robin in the quiet glen
Hidden from fame and all the strife of men
Sings unto time a pastoral and gives
A music that lives on and ever lives
Both spring and autumn years rich bloom and fade
Longer then songs that poets ever made
And think ye these times play things pass proud skill
Time loves them like a child and ever will
And so I worship them in bushy spots
And sing with them when all else notice not
And feel the music of their mirth agree
With that sooth quiet that bestirreth me
And if I touch aright that quiet tone
That soothing truth that shadows forth their own
Then many a year shall grow in after days
And still find hearts to love my quiet lays

John Clare

Birds and Spring

The happy birds in their delight bring home
To our doors the news that spring is come
Eave haunting sparrow that no song employs
Pull off the apple blooms for very joys
And that delightful neighbour ever merry
The robin with a bosom like a cherry
Comes to the threshold welcome pert and bold
Where crumbs lay littered when the day was cold
And whistles out so loud the folks within
Jump with surprise and wonder at the din
And when they run to see supprise will smile
Scarcely believing Robins sound so loud
But spring is come and he is overproud
To see young leaves that nothing comes to spoil.

John Clare, from *The Midsummer Cushion* (c.1833)

from *The Autumn Robin*[38]

Sweet little bird in russet coat
 The livery of the closing year
I love thy lonely plaintive note
 And tiny whispering song to hear
While on the stile or garden seat
 I sit to watch the falling leaves
Thy songs thy little joys repeat
 My loneliness relieves.

And many are the lonely minds
 That hear, and welcome thee anew
Not taste alone, but humble hinds
 Delight to praise and love thee too
The veriest clown beside his cart

---

[38]   I have omitted verses 5–7 and 10–14.

Turns from his song with many a smile
To see thee from the hedgerow start
To sing upon the stile

The shepherd on the fallen tree
Drops down to listen to thy lay
And chides his dog beside his knee
Who barks and frightens thee away
The hedger pauses ere he knocks
The stake down in the meadow gap
The boy who every songster mocks
Forbears the gate to clap

When in the hedge that hides the post
Thy ruddy bosom he surveys
Pleased with thy song in pleasure lost
He pausing mutters scraps of praise
The maiden marks at days decline
Thee in the yard on broken plough
And stops her song to listen thine
While milking brindled cow

Domestic bird thy pleasant face
 Doth well thy common suit commend
To meet thee in a stranger place
 Is meeting with an ancient friend
I track the thickets glooms around
 And there, as loath to leave agen
Thou comest, as if thou knew the sound
 And loved the sight of men

The loneliest wood that men can trace
 To thee a pleasant dwelling gives
In every town and crowded place
 The sweet domestic Robin lives
Go where we will in every spot
 Thy little welcome mates appear
And, like the daisies common lot
 Thou'rt met with everywhere

And could my notes steal aught from thine
 My words but imitate thy lay
Time would not then his charge resign
 Nor throw the meanest verse away
But ever at this mellow time
 He should thine autumn praise prolong
So would they share eternal prime
 With daiseys and thy song

John Clare

Sweet russet stranger welcome here
And may the mirth be long
How sweet at autumns closing year
To hear thy undersong
While on the garden bench I rest
Beneath the eldern leaves
And hear my little merry guest
Sing to the falling leaves

Thy unknown song how sweet to meet
By him who musing walks alone

Though humble hearts thy music greets
Tis not less sweet for being unknown
The far famed nightingale that shares
Praise in but every song
The popular voice of music heirs
And does thy anthem wrong

'Tis wrong that thou shouldst be despised
When these gay queens appear
They sing when summer flowers are prized
Thou at the closing year
Well let the heedless and the proud
Vaunt more exalted lays
The joy that thou from sorrow finds
Is more to thee than praise.

John Clare

The Red Robin

Cock Robin he got a neat tippet at spring
And he sat in a shed and heard other birds sing
And he whistled a ballad as loud as he could
And built him a nest of oak leaves by the wood
And furnished it just as the celandine pressed
Like a bright burning blaze by the edge o' its nest
All glittering with sunshine and beautiful rays
Like high polished brass or the fire in a blaze
Then sung a new song on the bend o' the brere
And so it kept singing the whole of the year
Till cowslips and wild roses blossomed and died
The red Robin sung by the old spring side

John Clare

from *The Gardener's Bonny Daughter*

She's sweeter than the first o' spring
More fair than Christmas roses
When robins by the hovel sing
Sweet smiles the maid discloses
Her hair so brown her eye so bright
As clear as the spring water
I'll go and have a word tonight
With the gardener's bonny daughter

John Clare

from *To Autumn*[39]

Where are the songs of spring? Ay, where are they?
Think not of them, thou hast thy music too, -
While barred clouds bloom the soft-dying day.
And touch the stubble-plains with rosy hue;
Then in a wailful choir the small gnats mourn
Among the river sallows, borne aloft
Or sinking as the light wind lives or dies;
And full-grown lambs loud bleat from hilly bourn;
Hedge-crickets sing; and now with treble soft
The redbreast whistles from a garden-croft;
And gathering swallows twitter in the skies.

John Keats (1795-1821)

from *An Autumn Eve: An Epistle to my Brother James*

The day drew quickly to a close,
And all in nature sought repose;
No music on the ear arose
        From warbling throats,
Save where the robin midst the boughs
        Tun'd his last notes.

Robert Kerr (1811-1848)

---

[39]   This is the last of the three verses of this ode, one of the best known of all English poems. The robin has such a hold on the British imagination that most readers, if asked what Keats refers to, will remember the robin, although only a single line, but anything else only with difficulty.

Chapter 6
'Lord in Heaven, how he Sings!'

After about 1840, the poems on robins singing change in character again. Although there is still some serious melancholy, many of the autumn references become more positive and the season celebrated largely moves to winter. Home comforts had increased further with the industrial age and this allowed a fuller appreciation of this hardest time of year. As the twentieth century progressed into the twenty-first, poems on the robin's song become more general and some of the poems give the robin a mainly symbolic meaning. Some poets have found the song unsettling, reflecting these unsettled times.

The poem by Peter Walton in this chapter mentions singing at night. This has been much reported recently and is usually thought to be associated with street lights. Some records are reported in *Birds Britannica* (2005, ed. Mark Cocker and Richard Mabey). Although it is likely to have increased with the great increase in street lighting[40], it is evidently not a new phenomenon:

> Everyone knows that robins sing all night.
>
> R.D. Blackmore (1825-1900), from *Lorna Doone* (1869)

This is the earliest definite reference I have found[41]. The habit may have caused it to be mistaken for a nightingale: was it actually a robin that '… sang in Berkeley Square' in the popular 1920s song? And was it really a 'Blackbird singing in the dead of night', in the Beatles' well-known song?

---

[40]   Recent research by Dr R. Fuller of Sheffield University has suggested that the more general noise there is during the day the more robins sing at night.

[41]   I am tempted to suggest that it is the reason that George Chapman referred to it as 'yellow autumn's nightingale' (see Chapter 3).

In the twentieth century, natural history books have often described the robin's song. Even these mostly refer to it as 'pensive' or 'melancholy', or similar. Its function is discussed in Chapter 8 but one writer wrote:

> 'In style, robin music is romantic and rather florid. His voice can be sweet and his sub-song is especially charming. When he uses song for disputing with other Robins his timbre often becomes shrill and he distorts phrases that in gentler moods are sung musically. Especially in autumn territorial battles, when song seems used as a language, certain phrases sound threatening, abusive, triumphant, etc.; according to how the battle with his opponent progresses....

'To me, the music of running brooks and fast-flowing hillside streams is suggested by Robin's sub-song....When singing this whispered sub-song, Robins often close their eyes and the sound seems to come from far away. At other times they may turn their head from side to side while singing this almost inaudible song, with the air of a public speaker addressing an audience.'

Len Howard, from Birds as Individuals (1952)

from *Enoch Arden*

Where either haven open'd on the deeps,
Roll'd a sea haze and whelmed the world in gray;
Cut off the length of highway on before,
And left but narrow breadth to left and right
Of withered holt or tilth or pasturage.
On the nigh-naked tree the robin piped
Disconsolate, and thro' the dripping haze
The dead weight of the dead leaf bore it down: ...

Alfred, Lord Tennyson (1809-1892)

Redbreast, early in the morning,
Dark and cold and cloudy grey,
Wildly tender is thy music,
Chasing angry thought away.

Emily Bronte (1818-1848)

'September 24th. – In the morning I rose, light and cheerful – nay, intensely happy. The hovering cloud cast over me by my aunt's views, and by the fear of not obtaining her consent, was lost in the bright effulgence of my own hopes, and the too delightful consciousness of requited love. It was a splendid morning; and I went out to enjoy it, in a quiet ramble, in company with my own blissful thoughts. The dew was on the grass, and ten thousand gossamers were waving in the breeze; the happy red-breast was pouring out its little soul in song, and my heart overflowed with silent hymns of gratitude and praise to heaven.'

Anne Bronte (1820-1849), from
The Tenant of Wildfell Hall

The Redbreast

On the yellow spray
He, like the white-haired prophet, sits alone,
A mourner among ruins, thro' the day
Making melodious moan.

While the wintry rime
Falls on his wings, the lone, last minstrel pours:
Wild fitful farewells to the sunny time,
Low requiems o'er the flowers.

Or, on lowly sheds
Thou sittest, voiceless with unmeasured woe,
While o'er the cold dead summer, winter spreads
A winding sheet of snow.

Give thy sorrow scope,
Or from the frozen bough or withered leaf
Speak soothingly, in whispers such as Hope
Breathes in the ears of Grief.

Sing the coming hours,
The warm, glad sheen of living spring foretell,

When happy children, laden with bright flowers,
Return from brook and dell.

So, thro' life's dull years,
The soul's unlovely winter, I from thee
May draw some solace, and thro' mists and tears
Gaze on the bright to be.

Ben Preston (1819-1902)

from *Winter*

And the flushed robin, in the evenings hoar,
Does of Love's Day, as if he saw it, sing.

Coventry Patmore (1823-1896)

Desolate

From the sad eaves the drip-drop of the rain!
The water washing at the latchel door;
A slow step plashing by upon the moor;
A single bleat far from the famished fold;
The clicking of an embered hearth and cold;
The rainy robin tic-tac at the pane.

'So as it is with thee
Is it with me,
So as it is and it used not to be,
With thee used not to be,
Nor me.'
So singeth robin on the willow tree,
The rainy robin tic-tac at the pane.

Here in this breast all day
The fire is dim and low,
Within I care not to stay,
Without I care not to go.

A sadness ever sings
Of unforgotten things,
And the bird of love is patting at the pane;
But the wintry water deepens at the door,
And a step is plashing by upon the moor
Into the dark upon the darkening moor,
And alas, alas, the drip-drop of the rain!

Sydney Dobell (1824-74) from *England in Time of War*

from *The Lover and Birds*[42]

Within a budding grove,
  In April's ear sang every bird his best,
But not a song to pleasure my unrest
  Or touch the tears unwept of bitter love;
Some spake methought with pity, some as if in jest.
              To every word
              Of every bird
      I listened, or replied as it behove.

'There's something, something sad
  I half remember' – piped a broken strain.
Well sung, sweet Robin! Robin sung again.
  'Spring's opening, cheerily, cheerily! be we glad!'
Which moved, I wist not why, me melancholy mad,
              Till now grown meek,
              With wetted cheek,
      Most comforting and gentle thoughts I had.

William Allingham (1824-1889)

---

[42]   This is the first and last of six verses, others transcribing the chaffinch,
blackbird, thrush and lark's songs.

To Robin Redbreast

Merrily 'mid the faded leaves,
O Robin of the bright red breast!
Cheerily over the Autumn eaves,
Thy note is heard, bonny bird;
Sent to cheer us, and kindly endear us
To what would be a sorrowful time
Without thee in the weltering clime:
Merry art thou in the boughs of the lime,
While thy fadeless waistcoat glows on thy breast,
In Autumn's reddest livery drest.

A merry song, a cheery song!
In the boughs above, on the sward below,
Chirping and singing the live day long,
While the maple in grief sheds its fiery leaf,
And all the trees waning, with bitter complaining,
Chestnut, and elm, and sycamore,
Catch the wild gust in their arms, and roar
Like the sea on a stormy shore,
Till wailfully they let it go,
And weep themselves naked and weary with woe.

Merrily, cheerily, joyously still
Pours out the crimson-crested tide.
The set of the season burns bright on the hill,
Where the foliage dead falls yellow and red,
Picturing vainly, but foretelling plainly
The wealth of cottage warmth that comes
When the frost gleams and the blood numbs,
And then, bonny Robin, I'll spread thee out crumbs
In my garden porch for thy redbreast pride,
The song and the ensign of dear fireside.

George Meredith (1828-1909)

from *Autumn Violets*

And, just so, recall the moments
When, beneath the minster clang,
We, ere yet we knew a sorrow,
With the robin-redbreast sang,
And the sound of childish laughter
Through the peaceful meadows rang.

Bessie Rayner Parkes (1829-1925)[43]

The Key-note

Where are the songs I used to know,
  Where are the notes I used to sing?
  I have forgotten everything
I used to know so long ago;
Summer has followed after spring;
  Now autumn is so shrunk and sere,
I scarcely think a sadder thing
  Can be the winter of my year.
Yet Robin sings through winter's rest,
  When bushes put their berries on;
While they their ruddy jewels don,
  He sings out of a ruddy breast;
The hips and haws and ruddy breast
  Make one spot warm where snowflakes lie,
They break and cheer the unlovely rest
  Of winter's pause – and why not I?

Christina Rossetti (1830 – 94)

---

[43] Parkes was a well-known political radical and Unitarian in her day; now perhaps remembered mainly for being the mother of Hilaire Belloc.

I wonder if the sap is stirring yet,
If wintry birds are dreaming of a mate,
If frozen snowdrops feel as yet the sun,
And crocus fires are kindling one by one?
Sing, Robin, sing!
I still am sore in doubt concerning spring

Christina Rossetti

Willow

The feathers of the willow
Are half of them grown yellow
Above the swelling stream;
And ragged are the bushes,
And rusty now the rushes,
And wild the clouded gleam.

The thistle now is older,
His stalk begins to moulder,
His head is white as snow;
The branches all are barer,
The linnet's song is rarer,
The robin pipeth now.

Richard Watson Dixon (1833-1900)

A Robin

Flame-throated robin on the topmost bough
  Of the leafless oak, what singest thou?
      Hark! He telleth how –
  'Spring is coming now; Spring is coming now.

Now ruddy are the elm-tops against the blue sky,
  The pale larch donneth her jewelry;
      Red fir and black fir sigh,
  And I am lamenting the year gone by.

The bushes where I nested are all cut down,
   They are felling the tall trees one by one,
       And my mate is dead and gone,
   In the winter she died and left me lone.

She lay in the thicket where I fear to go;
   For when the March winds after the snow
       The leaves away did blow,
   She was not there, and my heart is woe:

And sad is my song, when I begin to sing,
   As I sit in the sunshine this merry spring:
       Like a withered leaf I cling
   To the white oak-bough, while the wood doth ring.

Spring is coming now, the sun again is gay;
   Each day like a last spring's happy day.'
       Thus sang he; then from his spray
   He saw me listening and flew away.

Robert Bridges (1844–1930)

   The birds that sing on autumn eves[44]
   Among the golden-tinted leaves,
   Are but the few that true remain
   Of budding May's rejoicing train.

   Like autumn flowers that brave the frost,
   And make their show when hope is lost,
   These 'mong the fruits and mellow scent
   Mourn not the high-sunned summer spent.

   Their notes thro' all the jocund spring
   Were mixed in merry musicking:

---

[44] Although robins are not mentioned explicitly, this poem clearly refers
to them so I have included it.

They sang for love the whole day long,
But now their love is all for song.

Now each hath perfected his lay
To praise the year that hastes away:
They sit on boughs apart, and vie
In single songs and rich reply:

And oft as in the copse I hear
These anthems of the dying year,
The passions, once her peace that stole
With flattering love my heart console.

Robert Bridges

from *Fragments*

Meanwhile at times the manifold
Imperishable perfumes of the past
And coloured pictures rise on me thick and fast:
And I remember the white rime, the loud
Lamplitten city, shops, and the changing crowd;
And I remember home and the old time,
The winding river, the white moving rhyme,
The autumn robin by the river-side
That pipes in the grey eve.

Robert Louis Stevenson (1850-1894)

Robin's Water-Music

Scarce heard amid the choral throng
 That gave the spring its greeting,
You triumph, Robin, when your song
 Marks Summer's joys retreating;

Then, while the green leaves flame to gold,
  And rain drips on their embers,
You raise, above the sodden mould,
  The song of all Septembers.

Erratic, wistful, sweet, and shrill,
  The grave and gay you mingle,
As changeful as the trickling rill
  That voices glade and dingle,-
      From high to low,
      Now swift, now slow,
  Like water o'er the pebbles,
      Meandering here,
      And darting there,
  To sparkle in the trebles.

Chir'ri-tew! Iri'ri-tew!
  Wis'-yoo, Wis'-yoo!
  Wee'! – Swee'! – Tew-ay'!
Tew, tew', tew, Psee'!
  Chirri-wee'! Tyo-to'!
Se-Wis'sy-wissy, Wis'sy-wissy, Wee'!

Until in soft soliloquy,
  You enter realms more tender,
And drop from heights of ecstasy,
  A falling trail of splendour –
      Brilliant gems no casket treasures,
      Crystal tones no music measures –
  A glittering, flickering, tinkling streamlet,
  Fragile as a dream.

See, See', See, TSEE'…!
Choo-it'ty, Tu-it'ty, Choo-it'ty, Tu-it'ty, Choo-ee'!
    Wee-chee'! Wee-tsee'…!
Che-wir'rio, Ir'rio, Wir'-rio, Ir'-rio-ee'!

As rockets soar
Aloft to fall in twinkling disarray,
　　As fountains pour
To break adrift in showers of glistering spray.

Tit-it'! Tit-it-it-it'! Tit'! Tit'!
Yes, robin, yes! I must admit
(*Tit-it'-it-it'! Tit-it'-it-it!*)
　My actions were suspicious, –
For no true gardener stops his spade
To hear a little bird's cascade
　Of music, though delicious!
But when, enraptured, down the scale
　You dance by steps so slender,
　　　The Nightingale's *Tyo-tyo'-tyo-tew'*,
　　　The Throstle's *Tirra-lirra-loo,*
　　　Grow pale
Before your rich chromatic splendour.

Walter Garstang (1868-1949)[45], from *Songs of the Birds* (1935, 3rd edn.)

Robin Redbreast

Robin on a leafless bough,
　Lord in Heaven, how he sings!
Now cold winter's cruel wind
　Makes playmates of withered things.

---

[45]　This gloriously eccentric poem from a professor of zoology at Leeds is accompanied by a musical notation of the song (¾ time in C minor). He regards the robin as part of Oberon's choir and suggests that it is 'sounding all the heights and depths of the chromatic scale on his Chopinesque excursions.' The robin's song has received just three explicit transcriptions that I have found (the others being Dobell's and Allingham's earlier), though some others in this chapter suggest it. By contrast the nightingale and the thrush receive many.

How he sings for joy this morn!
  How his breast doth pant and glow!
Look you how he stands and sings,
  Half-way up his legs in snow!

If these crumbs of bread were pearls,
  And I had no bread at home,
He should have them for that song;
  Pretty robin redbreast, Come.

                    W. H. Davies (1871–1940)

In the Snow

Hear how my friend the robin sings!
      That little hunchback in the snow,
As it comes down as fast as rain.
      The air is cold, the wind doth blow,

And I, with heart as light as his,
      And to my ankles deep in snow,
Hold up a fist as cold as Death's,
      And into it I laugh and blow –
I laugh and blow my life's warm breath.

                    W.H. Davies

from The One Singer

No other sound is heard,
      Save from those boughs so bare –
Hark! Who sings that one song?
      'Tis Robin sings so rare.
How sweet! Like those sad tunes
      In homes where grief's not known;
Or that a blind girl sings
      When she is left alone.

                    W.H. Davies

Wee, Chir-ri - tew - ee - o, Tew - ee - o!

Tsee Wir-ri-o, Ir-ri-o, Wir-ri-o, Ir - ri - o - ee!

Winter

Clouded with snow
The cold winds blow,
And shrill on leafless bough
The robin with its burning breast
Alone sings now.

The rayless sun,
Day's journey done,
Sheds its last ebbing light
On fields in leagues of beauty spread
Unearthly white.

Thick draws the dark,
And spark by spark,
The frost-fires kindle, and soon
Over that sea of frozen foam
Floats the white moon.

Walter de la Mare (1873-1956)

Winter

Green Mistletoe!
Oh, I remember now
A dell of snow,
Frost on the bough;
None there but I:
Snow, snow, and a wintry sky.

None there but I,
And footprints one by one,
Zigzaggedly,
Where I had run;
Where shrill and powdery
A robin sat in the tree.

And he whistled sweet;
And I in the crusted snow
With snow-clubbed feet
Jigged to and fro,
Till, from the day,
The rose-light ebbed away.

And the robin flew
Into the air, the air,
The white mist through;
And small and rare
The night-frost fell
In the calm and misty dell.

And the dusk gathered low,
And the silver moon and stars
On the frozen snow
Drew taper bars,
Kindled winking fires
In the hooded briers.

And the sprawling Bear
Growled deep in the sky;
And Orion's hair
Streamed sparkling by:
But the North sighed low,
'Snow, snow, more snow!'

Walter de la Mare

from *Digging*

It is enough
To smell, to crumble the dark earth,
While the robin sings over again
Sad songs of autumn mirth.

Edward Thomas (1878-1917)

February

The robin on my lawn
Was the first to tell
How, in the frozen dawn,
This miracle befell,
Waking the meadows white
With hoar, the iron road
Agleam with splintered light,
And ice where water flowed:
Till, when the low sun drank
Those milky mists that cloak
Hanger and hollied bank,
The winter world awoke
To hear the feeble bleat
Of lambs on downland farms:
A blackbird whistled sweet;
Old beeches moved their arms
Into a mellow haze
Aerial, newly-born:
And I, alone, agaze,
Stood waiting for the thorn
To break in blossom white,
Or burst in a green flame ...
So, in a single night,
Fair February came,
Bidding my lips to sing
Or whisper their surprise,
With all the joy of spring
And morning in her eyes.

Francis Brett Young (1884-1954)

from *Baby Running Barefoot*

And the sight of their white playing in the grass
Is winsome as a robin's song, so fluttering;

D.H. Lawrence (1885-1930)

The Redbreast

The redbreast smoulders in the waste of snow:
His eye is large and bright, and to and fro
He draws and draws his slender threads of sound
Between the dark boughs and the freezing ground.

Anthony Rye, from *The Inn of Birds* (1947)

Any Small Robin

This little fellow, blood smeared on his breast,
Stands alone in a world of tumbling leaves,
The winds of autumn toss the gathered sheaves
And strip the secrecy from every nest.
The sun goes down storm-harried to the west,
And sinks defeated. Still young robin weaves
His tiny music, a pattern that achieves
Nothing; or so a cynic might have guessed,
But wait! That robin's song was overheard
By some heart-broken mortal at the end
Of all endurance; or it showered above
The clods late-shovelled over one revered
And mourned with grief impossible to mend,
Maybe the listener found new faith, new love.

Richard Church (1893-1972),
from *Lyrical Poems*, 1942-7

from *A Sedative at Daybreak*

The thrush, enlightener of the dark,
The blackbird demonstrating Bach,
The wren exploding into praise,
The chaffinch blissful with one phrase,
The curlew bubbling from a cloud,
The robin thinking thoughts out-loud,
The swift amazed at his own speed,
The starling glorified in greed,
The storm-cock pinnacled for shouting,
The tawny owl at dawn of doubting,
The thrush illumining the world,
The robin noting buds are pearled,
The blackcap's nimble sweet contralto,
The blackbird's almost human alto, ...

Later, the robin appears three further times:

The thrush irradiating day,
The robin commenting on May...

The ring-dove, rhythmic in a trance,
The robin's brief observant glance...

The nuthatch, flicking stones on ice,
The robin tempering sound advice...

Laurence Whistler (1912-2000),
from *The View from this Window* (1956)[46]

---

[46]   This long poem is a wonderful, dreamy description of dawn. The lines quoted are among 90 lines devoted to birds and the dawn chorus, and are reminiscent of John Skelton (Chapter 3)

December Song

On the eaves
A robin sings, with berry eyes
And breast redder than the dead leaves
Dangling his notes like beads,
A luminous, tinkling string.
A robin sings in the evening,
Under smoky December skies –
   And so would I sing.

In the sky
A star shines on the kerb of day.
The waking night from light-bleared eye
With one clear, glowing tear is weeping,
Dipping its lids to mine.
A star shines in the dusk
Not frosted yet by the Milky Way –
   And so would I shine.

Norman Nicholson (1914-1987),
from *Rockface* (1948)

Robin Song

I am the hunted king
 Of the frost and big icicles
  And the bogey cold
  With its wind boots

I am the uncrowned
 Of the rainworld
  Hunted by lightning and thunder
  And rivers.

133

I am the lost child
　　Of the wind
　　　　Who goes through me looking for something else
　　　　Who can't recognise me though I cry

I am the maker
　　Of the world
　　　　That rolls to crush
　　　　And silence my knowledge

Ted Hughes (1930-1998), from Crow (1972)

Robin

A robin is singing from the cottage chimney.
Departure means stepping through the sound-drapes
Of his pessimistic skin-and-bone aubade.
Household chores begin: wiping wet windows
For Venus in greeny solitariness, sky-coin,
Morning's retina; scattering from the wonky
Bucket immaterial ashes over moor grass
Turned suddenly redder at the equinox;
Spreading newspapers by the hearth for blackened
Hailstones. We have slept next to the whoopers'
Nightlong echoing domestic hubbub.
A watery sun glare is melting them.
His shadow on the lawn betrays the robin.
I would count the swans but it hurts my eyes.

Michael Longley (1939 -), from *Snow Water* (2004)

Mothers Never Die

It was a breeze less day
and the atmosphere was serene,
I was just listening to the ocean
when a Robin Redbreast
perched on my patio balcony,
She appeared to be surrounded
by a band of light,
but the balcony was in the shade,
Anyway; the little ball of feathers
nodded to me and I nodded back.

She chirped a couple of notes
to say hello
and I chirped back that I welcomed her,
I whistled a couple of lines of Amazing Grace

and her little head moved back and forth,
So I began to hum
and to my amazement she began to join in,
I stopped and let her take centre stage…
what a performance I was about to encounter.

She sang such a sweet serenade,
enchanting, enticing,
captivating my very soul,
She charmed me…
she had me under her wings,
I was spellbound,
Our souls connected
and although my eyes were wide open
we began to fly together,
Upward….upward… upward;
rising ever higher…higher…higher.

We began to glide on currents of air,
sail through clouds,
And all the time Amazing Grace
was being sung by my soul mate Robin,
I blinked a couple of times
and I was back on my chair
and Robin was perched on my shoulder
She whispered…
'Always respect others
and be a good boy'
That's what my mum always told me.

Michael Levy (1945 –),
written for International Women's Day, 2004

The Sub-Song [47]

I thought it a piece of fancifulness
When I first heard it mentioned:

The sub-song of the wintering bird:

but no, it's a scientific
classification of sound, denoting

a drowsily territorial
foreshadow, rehearsal or update,

sung past a leafless tree
in a minor key.

---

[47]   This poem is dedicated to Richard Mabey, who tells me that it arose
from reflections on a robin's autumn song.

With no particular
dedicatee.

Or recitative between arias,
summer and summer,

song of the slumbering, fixate
middle-comer.

I think I have caught the sub-song sounded
in various winter bars

by singletons with their beaks buried under

their shoulders, or in supermarkets,
wobbling alone a trolley,

with one wheel out of true:

far from the buzzard's mew
or the squawk of hawk on wrist,

crying, I fly, I can sing, I am here, I exist,
perpetually,

but it might have been nothing, or there again,
might have been me.

Kit Wright (1944 –),
from *Hoping It Might Be So* (2000)

Birdsong

Some trouble
Or other, two mornings running, stirred me
At four:
Too late for night, too early yet for day.
It was
Something I cannot now recall. But what
Afterwards
Kept me awake – though it had not woken me –
Was a bird,
Invisible; no stained breast, no pin-bright eyes,
Just the voice
Of all the robins I had ever heard
Or shall.

Peter Walton, from *Out of Season* (1977)

Chapter 7

The Robin in Myth and Folklore

In legends, myths and superstitions the redbreast appears again and again. These stories vary widely in different parts of the country and folklore notoriously gets modified through the years. Most of what we know was first written down in the nineteenth century when origins were already obscure[48]. Some of the better-documented stories are commented upon here.

The red of the breast is linked with fire in various accounts. The bird brought fire from heaven to man, or it tried to prevent a fire from going out. Or it tried to quench the fires of hell, or carried drops of water to moderate the temperature of the damned. The breast is red through its getting singed in the process. Such beliefs may go back to pagan times. There are versions of these stories from several countries as well as Britain.

> 'Nay' said Grandmother, 'have you not heard,
> My poor bad boy, of the fiery pit,
> And how, drop by drop, this merciful bird
> Carries the water that quenches it?
>
> 'He brings cool dew in his little bill
> And lets it fall on the souls of men;
> You can see the marks on his red breast still
> Of the fires that scorch as he drops it in.'

Anonymous (19th? century)

---

[48] The principal sources for the folklore and stories here are: Halliwell, J.O. (1849) *Popular Rhymes and Nursery Tales*, Dyer, T.F.T. (1884) *English Folk Lore*, Swainson, Rev. C. (1886) *The Folk Lore and Provincial Names of British Birds*, Ingersoll, E. (1923) *Birds in Legend, Fable and Folklore*, Opie, I. & Opie, P. (1955) *The Oxford Nursery Rhyme Book*, Graves, R. (1961) *The White Goddess*, and Cocker, M & Mabey, R. (2005) *Birds Britannica*.

It may be a relic of these stories that survives in a Cornish game, in which a stick is set on fire and whirled rapidly round with the words: 'Robin's alight, but if he goes out I will saddle your back.' The stick is passed from hand to hand, and anyone who lets the fire go out pays a forfeit. There is rather similar Scottish ritual.

Fire legends are told of other species with prominent red in their plumage and, more surprisingly, of the wren. The wren may be there simply because it is closely linked with the robin but, more likely, the identity is confused with the goldcrest, which has a flame on its head. The goldcrest was once known as the 'golden-crested wren' or 'little king'. The French, who have similar legends, use 'roitelet' for either species. Many stories make more sense with the goldcrest.

The red of the robin has caused it to be linked with blood, and so with disaster. This is mainly in relation to the capture or killing of robins:

> The blood on the breast of a robin that's sought
> Brings death to the snarer by whom it is caught.

Foretold disasters include not only death, but palsy or uncontrollable shaking of the hand. Household crockery may break, your house may be destroyed by lightning or fire or, strangest of all, your cows would give milk with blood in it. Such beliefs, like the fire legends, are also attached to other birds with red in their plumage.

The bad luck theme is taken up by a few more traditional rhymes:

> The robin and the redbreast
> The robin and the wren;
> If ye take out o' the nest,
> Ye'll never thrive again!

> The robin and the redbreast
>   The martin and the swallow,
> If ye touch one o' their eggs
>   Bad luck will surely follow.

More simply:

> If you go to catch a robin,
> Mind you don't come back a-sobbin'…

There is an ancient Celtic Yule festival, celebrating the eternal circle of the year, which ends with the robin, symbol or king of the New Year, defeating the wren, symbol of the old. This can be at the winter solstice, or St Stephen's day (26 December) or at the New Year itself. The wren may be ceremonially hunted and roasted or dismembered. A similar ritual may be the origin of the *Robin's Testament*, quoted in Chapter 2. These rituals are reported from France as well as country districts throughout the British Isles. The two birds have become associated with different trees: the wren usually with ivy, sometimes holly (evergreens for the declining year); the robin either with oak or birch (deciduous, so reborn for the new year).

A few superstitions have survived until recent times, for instance, a robin entering a house may be considered a bad omen, especially if accompanied by particular calls, but it can bring good luck at the New Year. On the other hand, several correspondents to *Birds Britannica* (2005) recorded robin incidents, especially entering the house when there had been a death. The robins have brought comfort, even if sometimes a slightly spooky comfort. These incidents reinforce the robin's association with death.

Other folk tales attribute the red of the robin to murdering its father. This, as illustrated in chapter 9, may not be far from the truth. More happily, it can be associated with love:

> In came the robin, and thus he said:
> 'I once loved a well-favoured maid;
> Her beauty kindled such a spark
> That on my breast I bear the mark.'

> Anonymous (18th century)

141

The robin can forecast the weather:

> If the robin sings in the bush
> Then the weather will be coarse;
> But if the robin sings on the barn,
> Then the weather will be warm.

This poor 'rhyme' is pessimistic: robins nearly always sing from a bush. It may have something to do with a sixteenth century song, reflecting the autumn song of the robin, which included:

> Robin Redbreast with his notes
> Singing aloft in the quire,
> Warneth to get you frieze coats,
> For winter then draweth near.

Anon., collected by William Wager (c.1566)

Woodcut by Thomas Bewick (1753-1828) from *British Birds* (1797)

One of the main themes in folklore of the robin is that it was regarded as sacred:

'the same redbreasts that we used to call God's birds.'

George Eliot (1819-1880),
from *The Mill on the Floss* (1860)

Inevitably, the wren joined in, and John Skelton referred to wrens as 'Our Lady's hens' in *The Lament for Philip Sparrow*, quoted in chapter 3. Some folk-rhymes collected during the nineteenth century have this theme, like:

> The robin redbreast and the wren
> Are God Almighty's cock and hen;
> The martin and the swallow
> Are God Almighty's birds to hallow.

Another version acknowledges the flying shape of the martins:

> Robinets and Jenny wrens
> Are God Almighty's cocks and hens.
> The martins and the swallows
> Are God Almighty's bows and arrows[49]

Another rhyme, from the West Country, states that:

> Wrans and robin-riddicks
> Tell all the cares o' God.

from *The English Dialect Dictionary*
(ed. J. Wright, 1904)

---

[49] A variation has 'The spink and the sparrow are the devil's bow and arrow'. It is interesting to note that the swallow is sacred, but the swift, often associated with the swallow, is the devil's bird in folklore.

A rather charming linking of the sacred and the blood stories comes from Finistère:

'*On assure que le bon Dieu l'appelle dans son paradis pour lui sucer le sang, lorsqu'il s'en trouve incommodé*

(One can be sure that God will call [a robin] in paradise to suck His blood when He is indisposed)

from E. Rolland, *Faune Populaire de la France*, vol ii, 1879

A legend that probably originated in Brittany, reaching Britain via Cornwall, tells that it acquired its red breast through trying to remove a thorn form Christ's crown of thorns on the cross. Alternatively, it flew down from the cross to comfort Mary.

Similar legends are told of other birds whose plumage contains red, including the crossbill, swallow and, especially, the goldfinch[50]. A goldfinch is regularly included in Renaissance Italian paintings of the Madonna and Child or the Crucifixion. It and the swallow were regarded as sacred to the Virgin. The robin does not appear in such pictures but the country rhymes quoted above, including those linking the robin with the swallow, may echo other stories.

The association with the cross was introduced into English and American literature early in the nineteenth century. I have found at least ten poems associating the robin with blood from the crown of thorns, all by minor nineteenth-century poets. Some American poets were evidently drawn to it, though most cannot have known the bird. Here is one example:

---

[50] The goldfinch frequently feeds on thistledown and the association with thorny plants as well as its red face makes it much more appropriate than the robin. It also has the great advantage of occurring in the Holy Land, whereas the robin does not!

The Robin Redbreast

Sweet Robin, I have heard them say,
That thou wert there upon the day
That Christ was crown'd in cruel scorn:
And bore away one bleeding thorn,

That so, the blush upon thy breast,
In shameful sorrow was impressed;
And thence thy genial sympathy,
With our redeemed humanity.

Sweet Robin, would that I might be
Bathed in my Saviour's blood like thee,
Bear in my breast, whate'er the loss,
The bleeding blazon of the cross;

Live ever, with thy loving mind,
In fellowship with humankind;
And take my pattern still from thee,
In gentleness and constancy.

Bishop George W. Doane (1799-1859)[51]

---

[51] Doane was a devoted bishop and occasional poet, as was his son, Bishop William Doane, who penned this pithy refutation of homeopathy in the late 19th century:

Stir the mixture well Lest it prove inferior, Then put half a drop Into Lake Superior. Every other day Take a drop in water, You'll be better soon Or at least you oughter.

The most attractive mention of all is the following imaginary episode about St. Columba on Iona. He, like other Irish saints, showed kindness to birds[52]:

> 'And Colum, sitting upon the strewed fern that was his bed, rubbed his eyes that were heavy with weariness and fasting and long prayer. On the ledge of the hole that was in the eastern wall of his cell he saw a bird. He leaned his elbow upon the leabhar-aifrionn[53] that was by his side. Then he spoke.
>
> 'Is there song upon thee, O bru-dhearg[54]?'
>
> 'Then the redbreast sang, and the singing was so sweet that tears came into the eyes of Colum, and he thought the sunlight that was streaming from the east was melted into that lilting sweet song. It was a hymn that the bru-dhearg sang, and it was this:

> Holy, Holy, Holy,
> Christ upon the Cross:
> My little nest was near,
> Hidden in the moss.
>
> Holy, Holy, Holy,
> Christ was pale and wan
> His eyes beheld me singing
> *Bron, Bron, mo Bron!*[55]

---

[52] Another delightful reference is in Adamnan's *Life*, written in the seventh century, about a crane that came exhausted to Iona. St. Columba saw that it was nursed and fed for three days and nights, until 'with renewed strength it was able to fly back to the pleasant part of Ireland from which it came'.

[53] A missal

[54] red-breast

[55] Grief, grief, O my grief!

Holy, Holy, Holy,
 'Come near, O wee brown bird!'
Christ spake: and lo, I lighted
 Upon the Living Word.

Holy, Holy, Holy,
 I heard the mocking scorn!
But *Holy, Holy, Holy,*
 I sang against a thorn!

Holy, Holy, Holy,
 Ah, his brow was bloody:
Holy, Holy, Holy,
 All my breast was ruddy.

Holy, Holy, Holy,
 Christ's-Bird shalt thou be
Thus said Mary Virgin
 There on Calvary.

Holy, Holy, Holy,
 A wee brown bird am I:
But my breast is ruddy
 For I saw Christ die.

Holy, Holy, Holy,
 By this ruddy feather,
Colum, call thy monks, and
 All the birds together.

'And at that Colum rose. Awe was upon him, and joy.

'He went out and told all to the monks. Then he said
mass out on the green sward. The yellow sunshine was
warm upon his grey hair. The love of God was warm
in his heart.

'Come, all ye birds!' he cried.

'And lo, all the birds of the air flew nigh. The golden eagle soared from the Cuchullins in far-off Skye, and the osprey from the wild lochs of Mull; the gannet from above the clouds, and the fulmar and petrel from the green wave: the cormorant and the skua from the weedy rock, and the plover and the kestrel from the machar: the corbie and the raven from the moor, and the snipe and the bittern and the heron: the cuckoo and cushat from the woodland: the crane from the swamp, the lark from the sky, and the mavis and the merle from the green bushes: the yellowyite, the shilfa, and the lintie, the gyalvonn and the wren and redbreast, one and all, every creature of the wings, they came at the bidding.

'Peace!' cried Colum.

'Peace!' cried all the birds, and even the eagle, the kestrel, the corbie, and the raven cried 'Peace, Peace!'

'I will say the Mass,' said Colum the White.

'And with that he said the Mass. And he blessed the birds.

'When the last chant was sung, only the Bru-dhearg remained.

'"Come, O Ruddy-Breast," said Colum, "and sing to us of the Christ."

'Through a golden hour thereafter the redbreast sang. Sweet was the joy of it.

At the end Colum said, 'Peace! In the name of the Father, the Son, and the Holy Ghost.'

'Thereat Ardan the Pict bowed his head, and in a loud voice repeated –

'*Sith (shee)! Anainm an Arthar, 's an Mhic, 's an Spioraid Naoimh!*'

and to this day the song of the Birds of Colum, as they are called in Hy, is *Sith − Sith − Sith − an − ainm − Chriosd −*

' "Peace − Peace − Peace − in the name of Christ!" '

'Fiona MacLeod' (William Sharp) (1855 − 1905)
in *The Three Marvels of Hy*

Some more recent authors have added their own versions to these legends:

' "It'll be a fine Christmas" [said the old man].

' "Why?" asked the child.

' " 'Cos Robin's singing on a stump. If he'd been singing under yon berry bush Santa Claus 'd have had to carry his umbrella." …

' "How does Robin know about the weather before anybody else?" he demanded.

' "Because he's God's own bird," said the old woman simply.

[She then relates how, when Jesus was a boy, a bit of grit went into Mary's eye and a robin noticed and flew to a stream, filled his beak with clear cold water. Telling a swallow to come with him they returned to the Virgin, now blinded with tears].

'She felt the fanning of their wings about her face and tried to look up. At that the robin let the cooling water fall into her eyes to ease the burning pain and bade the swallow pass one of his long tail feathers under the lid to remove the grit.

'Then it was that Jesus turned and saw what was being done. And He blessed the robin and the swallow. So

they are God's own birds. That is why folk should never
rob their nests.'

W.R. Calvert (1882–?)
from *Watchers of the Wild* (1945)

The following is an extract from a long poem that mentions another strange story, perhaps related to the fire legends. This is the only record I can find of this, though it may, again, relate to some ancient belief:

from *The Complaint of Philomene*

Or as the redbreast birds
Whom pretty merlins hold
Full fast in foot, by winter's night
To fend themselves from cold.

Though afterwards the hawk
For pity let them scape,
Yet all that day they feed in fear,
And doubt a second rape.

And in the nexter night
Full many times do cry
Remembering yet the ruthful plight
Wherein they late did lie.

Even so this silly bird,
Though now transformed in kind,
Yet evermore her pangs forepast
She beareth still in mind.

George Gascoigne (1525?–77)

There is no evidence that the majority of educated people took any interest in natural history until the pioneering work of Gilbert White in the 1780s. Even by 1873, John Ruskin still lamented the state of observation when he delivered this lecture to the University of Oxford:

'One of the robin's very chief ingratiatory faculties is his dainty and delicate movement, - his footing it featly here and there. Whatever prettiness there may be in his red breast, at his brightest he can always be outshone by a brickbat. But if he is rationally proud of anything about him, I should think a robin must be proud of his legs. Hundreds of birds have longer and more imposing ones – but for real neatness, finish, and precision of action, commend me to his fine little ankles, and fine little feet; this long stilted process, as you know, corresponding to our ankle-bone. Commend me, I say, to the robin for use of his ankles – he is, of all birds, the pre-eminent and characteristic Hopper; none other so light, so pert, or so swift.

'We must not, however, give too much credit to his legs in this matter. A robin's hop is half a flight; he hops, very essentially, with wings and tail, as well as with his feet, and the exquisitely rapid opening and quivering of the tail-feathers certainly give half the force to his leap. Leaps, I say; and you check at the word; and ought to check: you look at a bird hopping, and the motion is so much a matter of course, you never think how it is done. But do thou think you would find it easy to hop like a robin if you had two – all but wooden – legs, like this?'

At a later stage in his lecture Ruskin continued:

'I said, just now, he might be at once outshone by a brickbat. Indeed the day before yesterday, sleeping at Lichfield, and seeing, the first thing when I woke in the morning, (for I never put down the blinds of my bedroom windows,) the not uncommon sight in an English country town of an entire house-front of very neat, and very flat, and very red bricks, with very exactly square windows in it; and not feeling myself in anywise gratified or improved by the spectacle, I was thinking how in this, as in all other good, the too much

152

destroyed all. The breadth of a robin's breast in brick-red is delicious, but a whole house-front of brick-red as vivid, is alarming.'

John Ruskin (1819-1900)
from *Love's Meinie. Three Lectures
on Greek and English Birds*(1873)[56]

The classical uniformity condemned by Ruskin was in marked contrast to the popular taste of the time. In a London room of the period described by Thomas Hardy:

'The decorations tended towards the artistic gymnastics prevalent in some quarters at the present day. Upon a general flat tint of duck's-egg green appeared quaint patterns of conventional foliage, and birds, done in bright auburn, several shades nearer to redbreast-red than was Ethelberta's hair.'

Thomas Hardy (1840-1928), from
The Hand of Ethelberta (1876)

The robin was always one of the best-known of birds, however, and we have already seen how some American writers had picked up on its sacred association. One visiting American was, perhaps stereotypically, enthusiastic:

---

[56] Ruskin also included the following gem, to summarise the state of natural history as he saw it:'In general, the scientific natural history of a bird consists of four articles, - first, the name and estate of the gentleman whose gamekeeper shot the last that was seen in England; secondly, two or three stories of doubtful origin, printed in every book on the subject of birds for the last fifty years; thirdly, an account of the feathers, from the comb to the rump, with enumeration of the colours which are never more to be seen on the living bird by English eyes; and, lastly, a discussion of the reasons why none of the twelve names which former naturalists have given to the bird are of any further use, and why the present author has given it a thirteenth, which is to be universally, and to the end of time, accepted.'

'It was in 1878, when crossing the mountains in Ireland upon the top of a stage-coach, that I had my first sight of robinet, and I am afraid that by my unrestrained enthusiasm I provided entertainment for the other passengers. One passenger in particular, a lady of mature years and angular features, seemed to regard my exhibition of sentiment with no favour. Happily a gentleman sat near me, a person of importance and education. I asked him if the robin redbreast was in that part of the country. He said it was a common bird. I then began descanting on the fact of his warm place in the affection of children. Just at that moment one of these dear birds showed itself on the roadside. Of course, my enthusiasm was now unbounded and my tongue was freely let loose. The angular lady found it too severe a task to restrain herself fully, – for the words, 'so unbecoming!' escaped her lips. I tried to redeem myself by attempting some compliments on Irish literature: 'Madam', said I, 'your robin redbreast dwells in legend and history. In tradition it has the most venerated place among the birds. So you see there is something to condone the absence of restraint in one who is receiving his first vision of the calendared saint.' I fancied that the features of my fellow-passenger had become a little less angular. But continuing, in the hope of deepening the impression made, I said: 'Like the insect embalmed in the casket of precious amber, I find the redbreast in the 'Fairy Queen' of your own ancient poet Spenser, who in his Kilcolman Castle sang: 'The ruddock warbles soft.' There was a pleasant flutter among the passengers; but my lady's standard of the proprieties were firmly adhered to, and a silent dignity maintained.'[57]

Samuel Lockwood (1819-1894)
in *Animal Memoirs* (1888)

---

[57] Doubtless she was irritated by the quotation being referred to the wrong poem.

154

To complete this chapter are a few poems/prose that celebrate aspects of the robin's appearance:

from *Freaks of Fashion*

Robin says: 'A scarlet waistcoat
  Will be all the wear,
Snug, and also cheerful-looking
  For the frostiest air,
Comfortable for the chest too
  When one comes to plume and pair.'

Christina Rossetti (1830–94)

A Robin

Ghost-grey the fall of night,
  Ice-bound the lane,
Lone in the dying light
  Flits he again;
Lurking where shadows steal,
Perched in his coat of blood,
Man's homestead at his heel,
  Death-still the wood.

Odd restless child; it's dark;
  All wings are flown
But this one wizard's – hark! –
  Stone clapped on stone!
Changeling and solitary,
Secret and sharp and small,
Flits he from tree to tree,
  Calling on all.

Walter de la Mare (1873–1956)

Late Autumn

The boy called to his team
    And with blue-glancing share
Turned up the rape and turnip
    With yellow charlock to spare.

The long lean thistles stood
    Like beggars ragged and blind,
Half their white silken locks
    Blown away on the wind.

But I thought not once of winter
    Or summer that was past
Till I saw that slant-legged robin
    With autumn on his chest.

Andrew Young (1885-1971), from *Winter Harvest* (1933)

'...the robins inquisitively approaching me and staring
at the immobile figure in the deckchair and at the pile
of books on the stool; beady-eyed robins with a knock-
kneed stance, miniature Lloyd Georges, impudent and
provocative.'

Richard Church (1893-1972),
from *The Voyage Home* (1964)

Robin

With a bonfire throat,
Legs of twig,
A dark brown coat,
The inspector robin
Comes where I dig.

Military man
With a bright eye
And a wooden leg,
He must scrounge and beg
Now the summer's by:

Beg at the doors,
Scrounge in the gardens,
While daylight lessens
And the grass glistens
And the ground hardens.

The toads have their vaults,
The squirrels their money,
The swifts their journey;
For him the earth's anger,
The taste of hunger.

And his unfrightened song
For the impending snows
Is also for the rose

And for the great Armada
And the Phoenician trader
And the last missile raider –
It's the only one he knows.

Hal Summers (1911-2006),
from *Tomorrow is my Love* (1978)

The Redbreast – inspired by an engraving by Thomas Bewick (see p. 142)

Like a reddish leaf
of green and brown
the robin in the falling snow
flies up and down.

From the coalhouse to the tub,
the pantry to the byre,
closer he flies, and brings
his little panting fire.

He hops through the wind
of flakes, flits in a trice
from step to kitchen window,
pecks its crystal ice.

His eyes are big and cheeky,
black in his tilted head.
Shanks flexed for flight,
he begs a crumb of bread.

He chose our dark and stony yard
to warble long and loud.
Why has he made us his?
Why do we feel so proud?

James Kirkup (1918-),
from *A Bewick Bestiary* (1971)

Flight

By day, the returning terror of swifts, the scream
Of the loop over leaf, the power-dive on to the thatch;
And the robin whose vivid gift is a tongue of flame
To startle the stone at your foot into lyrical speech.
By night, the approach of the bat, neurotic and odd,
A flicker of bony fingers here and there;
And the cool owl swimming in the blinded wood,
A big moth saying nothing in the grey air.

By day, the shuttle of colour, speed that belongs
To the shadow that drops like a stone, the jewel that soars.
By night, the suspicion, the mere innuendo of wings,
The hint of a fugitive shadow across the stars.

By day, *jubilate* of saints in the heart of the holly,
By night, the cry of the lost in the luminous valley.

Laurence Whistler (1912-2000),
from *In time of Suspense* (1940)

159

A Redbreast at the End of Summer

Drawn by my raking,
My cashing-in on summer's work,
My breaking the drought-filled clods
To crumbs, to thirsty dust,
And picking out the flints,
There came a bird;

Earth-camouflaged
The same dry brown from head to tail;
Bold as the shadows; the sunset
Miniatured in its gorget
That was edged with the colour
Of a cooling sky.

Peter Walton,
from *Out of Season* (1977)

Chapter 8
'The Westminster Wonder'

A broadsheet of 1695

In the year 1695, a robin caused a sensation by entering Westminster Abbey and spending several days perched mainly on the funeral platform of Queen Mary II, as her body lay in state. It became known as the 'Westminster Wonder' and was mentioned in many publications, some including a portrait of the bird. Some treated its appearance as a political omen. Naturally, the significance of the omen varied markedly with the views of the writer, as mentioned in the song reproduced here. In fact, it seems that the robin was simply seeking shelter from the snow:

> 'They have had but a very indifferent day for the procession from Whitehall to the Abbey, a great snow falling in the midst of it. One who comes now from the Abbey tells me that the ladies had but draggled trains by the time they got there.'

Letter from Mr Vernon to Lord Lexington, from *The Lexington Papers* (ed. H.M. Sutton, 1851)

A New Song upon the Robin Redbreast's attending Queen Mary's Hearse in Westminster Abbey

All you that loved our Queen alive,
　Now dead lament her fate;
And take a walk to Westminster,
　To see her lie in state.

Among all other glorious sights
　A wonder you may see;
A bird, or something like a bird,
　Attend Her Majesty.

Sometimes it hops, sometimes it flies,
　Then perches o'er the hearse;
Then strains its throat, and sings a note
　That's neither prose nor verse.

The tune is solemn, as if set
  To fit some doleful ditty;
In lamentation for the Queen,
  To move all hearts to pity.

A perfect bird it seems to be,
  In feathers, bill and wings;
Nor is there feathered creature else
  That hops and flies and sings.

But what bird 'twas not known, until
  One wiser than the rest
Affirmed that he a robin was
  And proved it by his breast.

I call it He, not She, because
  It sings and cocks its tail,
Which that no female robin doth
  I'll hold a pot of ale.

This bird abides about the hearse
  Most part of every day;
Nor can you fail to hear him sing,
  Unless the organs play.

For organ pipes, being wider much
  Than robin redbreast's throat
Their noise must needs be loud enough
  To drown one robin's note.

Some say this bird an angel is,
  If so, we hope 'tis good;
But why an angel? why forsooth,
  They say he takes no food.

But that the robin lives by meat
  Is true, without dispute;
For though none ever saw him eat
  Enough have seen him mute.

And that sometimes undecently
  Upon the Statue-Royal,
Which made some call him Jacobite,
  Or otherwise illoyal.

The papists say this bird's a fiend
  Which haunts Queen Mary's ghost,
And by its restless motion shows
  How her poor soul is tossed.

But why then is this pretty bird
  So lively, brisk and merry;
This rather proves the Queen at ease,
  And safe from Purgatory.

An old star-gazing taylor says
  This frolic bird proclaims
How glad all such as he would be
  To welcome home King James.

And Partridge, who can make both shoes
  And almanacks to boot,
Says by this bird assuredly
  Some plot is still on foot.

For having like an augur watched
  Which way he took his flight
The Robin flew on his left hand
  And not upon the right.

A bird once in Rome's capitol,
  Said all things shall be well,
And why this harm less robin should
  Bode ill I cannot tell.

All we can guess is from this bird's
  Appearing still alone
Which represents our King's sole case,
  Now his fair Queen is gone.

The robin may have lost his mate,
  So hath King William his,
And that he may well match again
  Our hearty prayer is.

reprinted in *Wit and Mirth*
(4th ed. 1719, with a tune)

Another connection with royalty, though this time not a real robin, comes in the most extraordinary speech, delivered by Thomas Coryate when presenting his travel book, *Crudities*, to Prince Henry, eldest son of James I, in 1611. The robin allusion comes from the crimson velvet binding of the book, which is now in the British Museum:

> 'Most scintillant Phosphorus of our British Trinacria, even as the crystalline dew, that is exhaled up into the air out of the caverns and spongy pores of the succulent earth, doth by his distillation descend, and disperse itself again....

> 'I wish by the auspicious obumbration of your princely wings, this senseless shell may prove a lively bird, whose bill with length and strength may reach and peck the very mountains of Arabia, and there nestle, increase and engender, and so breed more birds of the same feather, that may in future time be presented as novelties unto your heroical protection. In the meantime receive into your indulgent hand (I most humbly beseech your Highness) this tender feathered *redbreast*. Let his cage be your Highness' study, his perch your princely hand, by the support whereof, he may learn to chirp and sing so loud, that the sweetness of his notes may yield a delectable resonancy *Ultra Garamantas et Indos.*'

Thomas Coryate (?1577–1617)

If a public figure bore the name of Robert, he would often be nicknamed Robin.

The earliest record (in M R James, 1930, *Suffolk and Norfolk*) is in a fifteenth century manuscript about St. Robert of Bury, a boy who was murdered by the Jews in 1181. A robin becomes his symbol and, in addition, there is a picture of a man shooting an arrow by his body, perhaps an early reference to *Who Killed Cock Robin?*

Queen Elizabeth referred to Robert Devereux, Earl of Essex as her 'Robin', a name she had earlier used for Leicester. The following two verses are from a long 'bird poem', evidently written about Essex while he was high in the queen's favour. He was later executed after an unsuccessful uprising against her:

Of all the birds that flyeth with wing
  The robin hath no peer,
For he in field and house can sing
  And chant it all the year.
This Robin is a pretty one,
  Well formed, at point devise,
A minion bird to look upon,
  And sure of worthy prize.
His looks be brave, his voice full shrill,
  His feathers bravely pruned,
And all his members wrought at will,
  With notes full timely tuned.

The goose but gaggeleth in her gate,
  The cock he can but crow,
A thousand birds do nought but prate,
  And jangle where they go:
The lark and linnet singeth well,
  The throstle doth his best;
The Robin bears away the bell,
  And passeth all the rest.
He is familiar with a lord,
  And dreams where ladies are;
He can in house sing and record,
  When bush and brier is bare.

from *The Camden Miscellany* (Vol. iii, 1855)

The Earl himself wrote a poem using the robin allusion:

A Passion of my Lord of Essex

> Happy were he could finish forth his fate
> In some unhaunted desert, most obscure
> From all society, from love and hate
> Of worldly folks; there might he sloop secure,
> Then wake again, and give God ever praise,
> Content with hips, and haws, and brambleberry;
> In contemplation passing still his days,
> And change of holy thoughts to keep him merry;
> That when he dies, his tomb might be a bush
> Where harmless Robin dwell with gentle thrush.

Robert Devereux, Earl of Essex (1566 – 1601)

In the next reign, another 'robin', Robert Carr, Earl of Somerset, was a royal favourite. He married Lady Frances Howard, Countess of Essex, after she had obtained an annulment from her first husband on dubious grounds. Sir Thomas Overbury had strongly advised against the marriage but the pair managed to get Overbury into the Tower. He was then poisoned by Lady Frances, with or without her husband's help. They were convicted of the murder and lived in disgrace, despite gaining a royal pardon. All this was recorded by Michael Drayton in the revised edition of his poem *The Owle,* in 1619. In this poem, the robin or robinet is the Earl of Somerset while the Countess of Essex is appropriately symbolized by a wren, and King James I by an eagle[58]. The wren is explaining her policy to a friend:

---

[58]   The allusions are discussed by K.Tillotson and B.H. Newdigate in *The Works of Michael Drayton*, vol.ii, ed. J.W. Hebel (1941). There is also allusion to the fable in which the wren outsoared the eagle by perching on its back.

Whenas my fine and nimble Robinet
(Whilst each one seems as busy as a bee,
T'attire their sovereign, and none more than he),
Watcheth his time, and aptly when he finds,
That the small birds, according to their kinds,
Shrink, when the Eagle doubled strength assumes:
As he stands proudly rousing up his plumes,
Nor never dreams what treachery intends,
Up by his train the crafty bird ascends,
And in the deep down closely doth him hide:
For the great Eagle, betwixt strength and pride,
His poor small body not so much as feels;
And thus this bird the king himself beguiles,
And in this sort transported to the spheres,
His sovereign's counsels, and Jove's secrets hears.
And when the wearied Eagle can no more,
Fresh from his back he into Heaven doth soar;
And coming thence, doth all to me relate,
And by this means we two will rule the state.

Michael Drayton (1563-1631)

In the reign of Queen Anne, the Duke of Buckingham is said to have remarked that England was:

> 'governed by a dirty chambermaid, a Welsh attorney and a profligate wretch that had neither honour nor honesty.'

Quoted by Winston Churchill, *Marlborough: His Life and Times* from Capt. R. Parker's *Memoirs* (1746)

The 'profligate wretch' was Robert Harley, Earl of Oxford, often referred to as Robin the Trickster, or as 'robin redbreast', in political pamphlets. Abusive verses were written about Harley and others. There is no doubt that he was a political schemer and was held responsible for, in effect, betraying Marlborough's army on a battlefield by withdrawing support. It was a popular custom of the time to use beautiful birds and mammals to represent the dishonest or incompetent rulers of the country. In the following, admittedly unpleasant, poem William King describes how a lady (Queen Anne) had brought a dog (Marlborough), a cat (Godolphin) and a rook (Bolingbroke) into her service, and then:

from *Robin Red Breast with the Beasts*

> One lucky day, when she was walking
> In her woods with servants talking,
> And stopped to hear how very well
> A Redbreast sang, then him to dwell
> With her she called: He came and took
> His place next to a favourite Rook,
> When Robin soon began to sing
> Such songs as made the house to ring;
> He sung the loss and death of sheep
> In notes that made the lady weep:
> How for his charge the Dog unfit,
> Took part with foes, and shepherds bit;
> Ev'n from his birth he did him trace
> And showed him cur of shabby race.
> The Cat he sung, that none could match
> For venomed might or cruel scratch
> That from a witch transformed she came
> Who kittened three of equal fame.

William King (1663–1712)

Eventually the dog and cat are furious and the queen turns the bird out, but still 'Robin does for her his care and zeal express'. William King wrote another poem on this theme, *The Eagle and the Robin*, and there are various anonymous works, mostly anti-Harley, though a few in favour. One more example:

from *She-land and Robinocracy*:

For Robinocracy consists
In getting power and gold
By any method that one lists
Which for the time will hold.

Anonymous, from *A Pill to Purge State Melancholy*
(1715)

The next Robin was Sir Robert Walpole, to whom there are several robin references, most of them tediously sycophantic[59]. A pamphlet of 1730 provides an example. This has its first nine verses about seasons and some birds and appears to be a nature poem. It continues:

from *The Robin*[60]

Summer invites some birds to sing,
  Some chirp it in the fall:
Each tries its melody in spring;
  But Robin sings in all.

The fiercest heats and cold, secure,
  Their impotence employ;
He can the winter's rage endure,
  The summer smiles enjoy,

No morning fair, but what's begun
  By Robin's tuneful lay,
He warbles to the setting sun,
  Yet rises with the day.

---

[59]   There were a few other political 'robins' of less interest around that time.

[60]   The original has capital letters and italics in various places. Robin is always in bold capitals.

With no resplendent plumage drest,
  His decent wings we see;
His beauty's chiefly in his breast,
  Where wise men's ought to be.

Thro' every change of good and bad
  Vicissitude can't harm;
Each black bird and canary's sad,
  When Robin still can charm.

The birds of prey, by Rapine taught,
  Are only wife for gain,
And nature, in a seeming fault,
  Bestows more power than brain.

Snares, guns, and craftsmen here employ;
  But Robin's each man's friend;
And where 'tis pastime to destroy,
  'Tis folly to intend.

The kite and buzzard may explore
  The spoils of victim mice;
But who prefers the owl before
  The bird of paradise?

Jove's eagle may, with tow'ring wings,
  To his own throne aspire;
But the instructive fable sings,
  The prudent wren rose higher.

This bird, as annalists relate,
  Our country could restore;
A wren secured half Britain's fate,
  A Robin now does more.

Anonymous (1730)

This gives yet another twist to the robin/wren pairing. The poem explains it in a footnote:

> 'There's an old tradition among the native Irish, that the wren, by fluttering upon the drums of the English, alarmed them in their camp, which prevented the design of the approaching Irish, who by surprise intended to have defeated and extirpated the English. On this account, 'tis a custom, that the common Irish, over the whole Kingdom, celebrate to this day, an anniversary persecution of the wren.'

At a time when Scotland was politically weakened and culturally dominated by the Act of Union with England, Allan Ramsay (1686-1758) wrote a poem, *The Eagle and Robin Redbreast, A Fable*. The poem advocates the Scottish cause, represented by the eagle. The robin pleases the kingly eagle with its song. The eagle tells the buzzard to reward it but the buzzard (referred to as Judas) then treats the robin very badly.

One other political pamphlet, published in 1819, is worth mentioning. It was written on behalf of those meeting at Manchester ('Peterloo'), in support of parliamentary reform of the protectionist agricultural laws, the notorious Corn Laws. Military forces were called out to break them up. The pamphlet starts:

Who killed Cock Robin? A satirical Tragedy, or Hieroglyphic Prophecy on the Manchester Blot[61]

Question: Who killed poor Cock Robins,
L-ES and others,
Fathers, sisters, children,
Friends and brothers?

Answer: We, said the Bold Sparrows
To their neighbours;
We did it with our sharpened
Yeomanry sabres.

Anonymous (1819)

Ebenezer Elliott was one of the best-known poetic advocates of the reform, referring to all the protectionist laws in his political poetry, very popular at the time. He became known as the 'Corn-Law Rhymer'. But his last poem was all about robins, not politics:

Thy notes, sweet Robin, soft as dew
Heard soon or late are dear to me;
To music I could bid adieu
But not to thee.

---

[61] The enduring appeal of *Who Killed Cock Robin?* has inspired other parodies, including, e.g. *Don't you know Cock Robin?* of 1850 written against a Birmingham police sergeant, and *Who'll Kill Inflation?* in the 1948 *Report to the Nation no. 13.*

When from my eyes this lifeful throng
Has passed away, no more to lie;
Then, autumn's primrose, Robin's song,
    Return to me.

Ebenezer Elliott (1781-1849)

Another political reformer, this time incorporating a travelling robin into his poem, was Edward Rushton. Born in Liverpool, he went to sea first at the age of 11 and, at 19, went on a slave ship. He was so appalled at the treatment of slaves that he helped them and, in so doing, picked up contagious opthalmia and went blind. He campaigned vigorously for the rest of his life against all aspects of the slave trade and the naval press gangs.

About a Robin

Poor bird! 'tis strange that thou shouldst roam
So far from thy sequestered home;
Shouldst leave the pure, the silent shade
For all this filth, this crash of trade.

Sweet are thy notes, yet minds intent
On life's prime object – cent per cent
Heed not thy soft, delicious strain,
Nor any notes, save notes of gain.

Sweet are thy notes, and yet I fear
Thou hast a dull and tasteless ear;
Else why forsake the lonely glen
For this deafening din of men;
The rattling cart, the driver's bawl,
The mallet's stroke, the hawker's call,
The child's shrill scream, the windlass song
As slow the vessel moves along,

All these commixed with many a harsh sound more,
Rise to thy bleak abode in one discordant roar.

Oh! Ruddock! Couldst thou name some shore
By British trade uncursed before,
Where Afric's injured race would come,
In crowds, for half the present sum;
Or couldst thou aid the speculating throng
The great commercial few would praise thy song.

Edward Rushton (1756-1814)

Red uniforms have led to several groups of people being called redbreasts or robins. The Fifth (Royal Irish) Lancers and, subsequently, the New South Wales Lancers, acquired the nickname as did the 'Bow Street Runners', precursors of the modern police force. These were well-known to fraternise with the criminals and lawyers, only arresting anyone when forced by circumstances to do so:

'I remember them very well as standing about the door of the office in Bow Street. They had no other uniform than a blue dress-coat, brass buttons (I am not even now sure that that was necessary), and a bright red cloth waistcoat. The waistcoat was indispensable, and the slang name for them was 'redbreasts', in consequence. They kept company with thieves and the like, much more than the detective police do.

Charles Dickens (1812-1870), in a letter to Walter Thornbury in *The Letters of Charles Dickens*, 1880

Currently three professional football teams are known as robins, all because of their red shirts: Bristol City, Cheltenham Town and

Swindon Town, and a few other amateur and junior teams have also adopted the name. Most have incorporated a robin into their logos. In this context, the car manufacturer, Reliant, brought out a succession of three-wheeled vehicles, one of which in the 1970s was called the Robin. The name was presumably coined to denote a domestic vehicle, and has become associated with all of Reliant's three-wheelers. It has been the butt of many jokes.[62]

In the sixteenth century, the red of the robin led it to be associated with gold.[63] By tradition gold is 'red', and 'ruddock', the old word for a robin, came to be used for a gold coin:

---

[62]   Q: What do you call a robin at the top of a hill? A: a miracle.
[63]   Goldfinch, yellowhammer and canary have also been names for gold coins.

Of Two Desperate Men

A man in deep despair, with hemp in hand,
Went out in haste to end his wretched days,
And where he thought the gallow tree should stand
He found a pot of gold: he goes his ways
Therewith eftsoon, and in exchange he left
The rope wherewith he would his breath bereft.
The greedy carl came within a space
That owned the gold, and saw the pot behind
Where ruddocks lay, and in the ruddocks' place
A knotty cord, but ruddocks could not find:
He caught the hemp and hung himself on tree,
For grief that he his treasure could not see.

George Turbevile (1540?–1610)

Ben Johnson, in this praise of riches, combines two meanings: that of redbreast as the bird, with that of redbreast as gold.

Jacques, counting over his gold

O in what golden circle have I danced?
Millaine these odorous and enflowered fields
Are none of thine. No, here's Elysium,
Here blessed ghosts do walk, this is the court
And glorious palace where the God of gold
Shines like the sun, of sparkling majesty;
Oh my fair feathered, my red-breasted birds,
Come fly with me, I'll bring you to a choir
Whose consort being sweetened with your sound,
The music will be fuller, and each hour
These ears shall banquet with your harmony.

Ben Jonson (1573–1637) from *The Case is Altered*

178

Firearms, both static and hand-held, have been named after birds. The best known of these is the 'musket', originally the name for the male sparrowhawk. Others were the 'saker', 'falcon' and 'falconet', all birds of prey, and 'robinet' for a half to one pound 'culverin' or cannon. In view of the others, this surely must refer to the male hobby, known at one time to falconers as a robin or robinet (page ix), although the robin is such a fighter that it might seem appropriate. Thomas Shelton, whether by accident or design, clearly confused the two:

from *Don Quixote*

'Stepping a little back, she (Dulcinea) fetched a rise, and clapping both her hands upon the ass's crupper, she lighted as swift as a hawk upon the pack-saddle, and sat astride like a man. Then said Sancho: "By Saint Roqui! Our mistress is as light as a robin-ruddock, and may teach the cunningest Cordovan or Mexicanian to ride on their genets." '

English translation of M. Cervantes by Thomas Shelton
(1620)

The word that Shelton translated into 'robin-ruddock' was from the Spanish *alcotán*, meaning a hobby, or 'robin' but not 'ruddock'. Shelton substituted the robin redbreast, an apt alternative, as it hops so lightly.

To complete this chapter, we return to some real robins that achieved fame through friendship with a great, though controversial, statesman:

'This is an age of curiosity. There is a desire to know about the private life of people who are much before the public; and birds, as well as men and women, are the subject of more curious and particular observation than they ever endured before. My own experience has been mainly with robins. Several of these were tamed at different times, not with any intention of scientific observation, but solely for the pleasure of being on terms of intimacy with birds in a free and natural state.'

Viscount Grey of Fallodon (1862-1933),
from The Charm of Birds (1927)

Grey was Foreign Minister from 1905-1916, and was perhaps the most important influence for taking Britain into the disastrous First World War[64]. When he took office, he had to give up country life and he longed to return to it. When he finally retired, his eyesight had almost gone, so that he could scarcely see the birds that he loved.

Grey was educated, like so many politicians, at Oxford University. He was once sent down for idleness as an undergraduate, but returned as Chancellor! His memorial is an institute for the study of birds. The creation of the Edward Grey Institute of Field Ornithology in 1938 would have pleased him. He had excited the anxious speculation of Europe through spending a day showing birds to an ex-President of the United States – a walk through the New Forest, with Theodore Roosevelt in June 1910. David Lack was the Institute's director from 1945 to 1973.

Grey wrote much about his robins, of which this is one short section:

'In estimating the difference between spring and autumn songs allowance must be made for the human mood and expectation of the mind. In autumn, when

> The warm sun is failing,
> The bleak wind is wailing,

when
> The chill rain is falling,
> The nipped worm is crawling,

---

[64] Some commentators have related this to aspects of his, often unhappy, life and have attributed a death-wish to him, but he was instrumental in forming the League of Nations afterwards.

and the sun is getting lower and the days shorter, our own minds are attuned to a minor key, and we find it in the robin's song. On a warm April day, when sap is rising and we are full of anticipation, with ears a-tiptoe for the first note of a blackcap, we judge the robin's song differently. "We used," said a Conservative, who was cutting my hair soon after the war, "to think of Mr Lloyd George everything that was bad. Now we admire him. Is it he or is it we that have changed?" And so I ask, listening to a robin in spring and comparing the impression remembered of the autumn, "Is it the song or is it I that have changed?" '

Viscount Grey of Fallodon

Viscount Edward Grey with one of his tame robins;
photo taken shortly before his death in 1933

With thanks to the Edward Grey Institute

181

Chapter 9
The Robin's Home Life

Maid Marian in the greenwood sighed:
    'If my man Robin were but a bird-Robin, how
        happily would we lilt among the leaves.'

Alfred, Lord Tennyson (1809-1892), from *The Foresters*

In Verona Valentine asked his servant, 'How know you that I am in love?':

'Marry, by these special marks: first, you have learned, like
Sir Proteus, to wreathe your arms, like a malcontent; to
relish a love-song, like a robin redbreast; to walk alone,
like one that had the pestilence; to sigh, like a schoolboy
that had lost his ABC; to weep, like a young wench that
had buried her grandam; to fast, like one that takes diet;
to watch, like one that fears robbing; to speak puling,
like a beggar at Hallowmass.'

William Shakespeare (1564 – 1616)
in *Two Gentlemen of Verona*

From *The Court of Love*

The second lesson robin redbreast sang,
'Hail to the god and goddess of our lay!'
And to the lectern amorously he sprang:-

'Hail' quoth he eke 'O fresh season of May,
Our mon(e)th glad that singen on the spray!
Hail to the flowers, red and white, and blue,
Which by their virtue make our lust(e)s new.'

Anonymous, c. 1540, from
Chaucerian and other Pieces (ed. W.W. Skeat, 1897)

Why the robin sings, indeed why any bird sings, is a subject of much interest. It undoubtedly performs more than one role. But the main role for the robin is not love, but war. The song and the red breast are, first, signals to rivals, though Tennyson was wrong to state that:

'In the spring a fuller crimson comes upon the robin's breast.'

Alfred, Lord Tennyson, from *Locksley Hall*

This may relate to an earlier idea, equally incorrect, that the cock robin is a brighter red than the hen. Even the great John Ray (1627-1705) repeated this error in his *Ornithology of Francis Willughby* (1678). The fact that robins are fiercely territorial did not totally escape classical writers:

'One bush does not shelter two robins'

Zenodotus (3rd century B.C.)

is known as a proverb. Some continental writers took up the theme:

'It has a peculiarity that it cannot abide a companion in the place where it lives and will attack with all its strength any who dispute this claim.'

G.P. Olina (1585-1645), from
Uccelliera (Manual of Birds) (1622)

In Britain, it was Oliver Goldsmith who first used the word territory to define a bird's defended area. W.H. Auden referred to:

...the plucky robin's canton...

W.H. Auden (1907-1973), from *Spain* (1937)

There were no writings on territory in robins until the nineteenth century. John Clare, in a letter to Messrs Taylor and Hessey, had clearly watched robins carefully and it was also taken up by Eliza Cook:

'It is not commonly known that the Robin is a very quarrelsome bird. It is not only at frequent warfare with its own species but attacks boldly every other small bird that comes in its way and is generally the conqueror. I have seen it chase the house sparrow which tho a very pert bird never ventures to fight it, hedge sparrows linnets and finches that crowd the barn doors in winter never stands against its authority but flyes from its interferences and acknowledge it the cock of the walk and he always seems to consider the right of the yard as his own.'

John Clare (1793-1864)

All saucy and rude as thou are,
Strutting up in thy *warrior* red.

Eliza Cook (1812-1889), from *Winter is Here*

Twentieth-century writers are somewhat rueful about the knowledge:

from *Birds all singing*

Something to do with territory makes them sing,
Or so we are told – they woo no sweet and fair,
But tantalise and transfigure morning air
With coarse descriptions of any other cock bird
That dare intrude a wing
In their half-acre – bumptious and absurd.

Come out and fight, they cry, and roulades of
Tumbling down sweetness and ascending bliss…

Norman MacCaig (1910-1996),
from *Riding Lights* (1955)

The Truth

Since I have seen a bird one day,
His head pecked more than half away;
That hopped about with but one eye,
Ready to fight again, and die –
Oftimes since then their private lives
Have spoilt that joy their music gives.

So, when I see this robin now,
Like a red apple on the bough,
And question why he sings so strong,
For love, or for the love of song;
Or sings, maybe, for that sweet rill
Whose silver tongue is never still –

Ah, now there comes this thought unkind,
Born of the knowledge in my mind:
He sings in triumph that last night
He killed his father in a fight;

And now he'll take his mother's blood –
The last strong rival for his food.

W.H. Davies (1871-1940)

It clearly shocked the children's writer, Frances Hodgson Burnett. After finishing the classic story, *The Secret Garden* (Chapter 11), she observed the robin that had been the inspiration for that story when seeing a rival:

'He flew at him, he beat him, he smacked him, he pecked him, he shrieked bad language at him, he drove him from the branch – from the tree, from one tree after another.... I was so frightened that I felt quite pale.'

Frances Hodgson Burnett (1849-1924),
from My Robin (1913)

It has become well-known as a fighter, and the leading popular science journal, the *New Scientist*, entitled an article 'Robin the red-breasted thug' (R. Harrow, 1994). It was as a fighter that the robin featured at the beginning of the hugely successful film *Gladiator* (2000). The Roman general Maximus, played by Russell Crowe, is longing to go home but is contemplating yet another battle to maintain Roman territory. This one is against the Germanic barbarians in the northern woods. A robin sits on a twig beside him and, watching it fly off, he resolves to fight. The robin here is perhaps playing a dual role: as the fierce defender of woodland territories, and as the domestic bird reminding the general of home (though it is only the domestic bird in Britain and, by extension, Hollywood – in Italy, they have been more ready to eat it).

It is the red of a robin's breast that provokes attack and robins can be indiscriminate:

'[A robin] came in twice yesterday, and flew about the room in an excited and enquiring manner. He began by flying towards me on the sofa, and made a circuit nearly round my head. I felt flattered, and thought it was a mark of attention from my little friend. But the second time another person was on the sofa, and I am inclined to think that the attraction was a tall figure of Dante's Beatrice hanging over the sofa. She is clothed in a long flowing garment of bright scarlet over a white tunic, and stands against a bright sky.'

J.M. Hayward, from *Bird Notes* (c.1890)

'Establishing a territory is a major part of attracting a female:

The unmated cocks sing in isolated territories and the hens come to them there. The cocks do not leave their territories in search of the hens...

The first stage of pair-formation in the robin is characterized by both threat postures and the loud singing typical of aggressive behaviour.'

David Lack (1910-1973), from *The Life of the Robin* (1943)

David Lack also pointed out that robins can form pairs as early as mid-December. Once the pair is formed the male will feed the female in what has become known as 'courtship feeding' and, later, will sing to his mate to bring her off the nest to be fed. Courtship feeding[65] was recorded by one lesser-known pastoral poet a century before it appeared in ornithological literature:

---

[65] See also Enid Blyton's *Sir Robin's Wooing* in Chapter 11

from *Walter and Jane*

E'en as the redbreast, sheltering in a bower,
Mourns the short darkness of a passing shower,
Then, while the azure sky extends around,
Darts on a worm that breaks the moistened ground,
And mounts the dripping fence with joy elate,
And shares the prize triumphant with his mate.

Robert Bloomfield (1766-1823)

A tame robin can also share with a human. The Duke of Argyll recounted to David Lack a remarkable occurrence at Inverary Castle, in the 1940s. Lady Elspeth Campbell had tamed a wild robin in the grounds so that it took food from her, and even visited her room. When confined to her room by illness, her tame robin visited her and, touchingly, presented her with worms.

Mrs Zoe Blundell, in Pinero's play *Mid-Channel*, calls her masculine attachments 'tame robins', but this is something of a libel. The robin is generally a faithful partner, although, as in all monogamous species that have been studied in detail, some 'cheating' goes on.[66] The anonymous compiler of *The Robin's Jubilee* of 1826 provided, at the start, a sequence of six poems on the robin's home life. The book takes what we today would consider an over-moralistic tone. Two extracts follow, one from the Preface, the other, the second poem of the sequence that starts the book:

> 'If our own race of bipeds would imitate to the full, the world would mend, for a rational man must always be ashamed to be outdone in virtue by a pair of simple Robins.'

The Robin's Nest

Why does my Bird, with crimson breast,
  Perch on the blooming plum-tree's bough,
That overshades his mossy nest,
  And no short pause from care allow?
But still retains the garden's way,
  Where broods in peace his faithful mate,
And sings for her his sweetest lay,
  Till day shuts in his evening gate?

What can this kind attention mean,
  While spring her beauties brings to cheer,
Till summer spreads the plenteous scene
  To bless the half-expiring year?
What is it all! but this to prove,
  Though sceptics dare the truth deny,
Nature's best gift's a soul for love,
  Enshrin'd in holy constancy!

Anonymous, from *The Robin's Jubilee* (1826)

---

[66] Dr David Harper of Sussex University estimates that up to a fifth of robins are bigamist.

The robin is notorious for its choice of nest sites, reports of which often find their way into local papers. The bird nests in niches and holes, which abound in woods but are scarce in gardens and villages. So it may be forced to choose a letter-box, discarded kettle, pump, or unmade bed, a 'pigeon-hole' in a desk, a human skull, the dead body of a cat... Here are a few of the more curious sites:

> 'His present majesty [William IV], when residing in Bushy Park, had a part of the foremast of the Victory, against which Lord Nelson was standing when he received his fatal wound, deposited in a small temple in the grounds of Bushy House, from which it was afterwards removed and placed at the upper end of the dining room, with a bust of Lord Nelson upon it. A large shot had passed completely through this part of the mast, and while it was in the temple a pair of robins had built their nest in the shot hole, and reared a brood of young ones. It was impossible to witness this little occurrence without reflecting on the scene of blood and strife of war, which had occurred to produce so snug and peaceable a retreat for a nest of harmless robins.'

> Edward Jesse (1780-1868) in
> *Gleanings in Natural History*

> 'A few years ago, a pair of robins took up their abode in the parish church of Hampton-in-Arden, Warwickshire, and for two years in succession affixed their nest to the church Bible, as it lay on the reading-desk. The worthy vicar would on no account have the birds disturbed, and accordingly introduced into the church another Bible, from which to read the lessons. A sacrilege, not so much on account of the daring liberty they had taken with the sacred volume, as for having plundered the rope-ends out of the belfry, wherewith to construct their habitation. Be this as it may, the old women of the village took it into their heads that the circumstance of

the robin's building on the Bible was highly ominous, and foreboded no good to the vicar. It so happened that he died in the month of June, of the second year of the bird's building in the church; an event which, no doubt, confirmed the old women in their superstition: '*Ni frusta augurium vani docuere parentes*' (Virgil)[67], and will be remembered and handed down to posterity, for the benefit of any future vicar, should the robins again make a similar selection.'

The Rev. W. T. Bree, from *London's
Magazine of Natural History* (1833)

When a robin built in the reading-desk of North Molton church, Devon, immediately under the Bible and prayer-book, it inspired:

Sweet social bird! confiding in our care,
Who here so oft frequents God's house of prayer,
Here sheltered from the hands of reckless youth,
Thy nest was built beneath the word of Truth.
How choice! How wise! May all who worship here
Now learn a lesson from thy fostering care,
Now follow in the path which thou hast trod,
And rear their young ones in the house of God;
Here train them in the way that they should go,
That with increasing years their peace may flow,
Till heaven at last be their eternal rest,
With Jesus and His saints for ever blest.

The Rev. W. Burdett, mid-19th cent., quoted by H.G.
Adams in *Our Feathered Families* (1862)

---

[67] 'Unless their deluded parents taught them augury in vain'
(from *The Aeneid*)

'A gentleman in my neighbourhood had directed one of his waggons to be packed with sundry hampers and boxes, intending to send it to Worthing, where he was going himself. For some reason, his going was delayed; and he therefore directed that the waggon should be placed in a shed in his yard, packed as it was, till it should be convenient for him to send it off. While it was in the shed, a pair of robins built their nest among some straw in the waggon, and had hatched their young just before it was sent away. One of the old birds, instead of being frightened away by the motion of the waggon, only left its nest from time to time for the purpose of flying to the nearest hedge for food for its young; and thus, alternately affording warmth and nourishment to them, it arrived at Worthing. The affection of this bird having been observed by the waggoner, he took care in unloading, not to disturb the robin's nest, and my readers will, I am sure, be glad to hear that the robin and its young ones returned in safety to Walton Heath, being the place from whence it had set out. Whether it was the male or female robin which kept with the waggon, I have not been able to ascertain; but most probably the latter, as what will not a mother's love and mother's tenderness induce her to perform? The distance the waggon went in going and returning could not have been less than one hundred miles.'

Edward Jesse (1780-1868) in *Gleanings in Natural History*

'Oddest of all is the robin who that same year [1939] nested behind the engine of an aeroplane in Denham. Six times the nest was destroyed by the human airman, and six times the feathered airwoman rebuilt it. Then the man gave in, and let her lay her six eggs in her seventh nest. The hatching of the eggs was odder still: Mrs Robin sat on her eggs till the plane went up, and while it soared in the sky the hot engine acted as foster mother. When it came down to earth, the patient robin took up her duties again. The young robins were hatched between flights, and each as it saw the light could boast that it had already out-soared the golden eagle.'

Eleanor Farjeon, from *The New Book of Days* (1941)

Robins can build fast, the record perhaps being one that built in a gardener's coat pocket between 9.15, when the man had hung up his coat in a shed and lunchtime, when the nest was almost complete. The robin has occasionally been reported ousting another bird from its nest, and even sharing a nest with a great tit or a pied wagtail. (Records from David Lack, *The Life of the Robin,* 1943).

William Turner, considered to be Britain's first ornithologist, described a robin's nest in 1544:

> 'It makes its nest among the thickest thorns and shrubs in Spineys, where it finds many oaken leaves, and when it is built covereth it with leaves, not leaving it open every way, but only one passage to it.'

William Turner (1508-1568), translated by John Ray in
Ornithology of Francis Willughby (1678)

This was much quoted by later writers (including Bewick) but actually records an unusual nest. Turner does say that it is a single observation remembered from his boyhood. In a letter John Clare described his observations on the nest:

> 'The Red breast frequently builds on the ground under the shelter of a knoll or stulp and its nest is often taken for that of the nightingales but it is easily distinguished from it as the robins is built with dead grass and moss on the out side while the Nightingale never forgets her dead oak leaves.'

John Clare, from a letter to Messrs. Taylor and Hessey

Despite what these writers say, normally a robin makes a cup-shaped nest with a foundation of dead leaves, and elsewhere Clare does describe the use of oak leaves.

For poems on the robin's nest, we can again turn to Clare, who described aspects of robins nesting in several poems:

from *The Robins Nest*[68]

Come luscious spring come with thy mossy roots
The weed strown banks – young grass – and tender shoots
Of woods new plashed sweet smells of opening blooms
Sweet sunny mornings and right glorious dooms
Of happiness – to seek and harbour in
Far from the ruder worlds inglorious din
Who see no glory but in sordid pelf
And nought of greatness but its little self
Scorning the splendid gift that nature gives
Where natures glory ever breathes and lives
Seated in crimping ferns uncurling now
In russet fringes ere in leaves they bow
And moss as green as silk – there let me be
By the grey powdered trunk of old oak tree

. . . .

Where moss grows old and keeps an evergreen
And footmarks seems like miracles when seen
So little meddling toil doth trouble here
The very weeds as patriarchs appear
And if a plant ones curious eyes delight
In this old ancient solitude we might
Come ten years hence of trouble dreaming ill
And find them like old tenants peaceful still
Here the wood robin rustling on the leaves
With fluttering step each visitor receives
Yet from his ancient home he seldom stirs
In heart content on these dead teazle burs
He sits and trembles oer his under notes
So rich – joy almost choaks his little throat
With extacy and from his own heart flows
That joy himself and partner only knows

---

[68]   I have omitted lines 15-59 of this long poem.

He seems to have small fear but hops and comes
Close to ones feet as if he looked for crumbs
And when the woodman strinkles some around
He leaves the twig and hops upon the ground
And feeds until his little daintys cloy
Then claps his little wings and sings for joy
And when in woodland solitudes I wend
I always hail him as my hermit friend
And naturally enough whenere they come
Before me search my pockets for a crumb
At which he turns his eye and seems to stand
As if expecting somthing from my hand
And thus these feathered heirs of solitude
Remain the tenants of this quiet wood
And live in melody and make their home
And never seem to have a wish to roam
Beside the ash stulp where in years gone bye
The thrush had built and taught her young to flye
Where still the nest half filled with leaves remains
With moss still green amid the twisting grains
Here on the ground and sheltered at its foot
The nest is hid close to its mossy root
Composed of moss and grass and lined with hair
And five brun-coloured eggs snug sheltered there
And bye and bye a happy brood will be
The tenants of this woodland privacy

John Clare

Red Robin

The sparrow seeks his feathers for a nest
And the fond robin with his ruddy breast
Hops round the garden wall where thickly twine
The leafing sweet briar and the propt woodbine
And in a hole behind the thickening boughs

He builds with hopeful joy his little house
Stealing with jealous speed the wool and hair
Were cows and sheep have lain them down to lair
And pecks the green moss in his murmering glee
From cottage thatch and squatting apple tree
Tutling his song –

John Clare

The bench beside the door is seen
For rest and up the wall the vine
Climbs thick the cot seems clad in green
On which the sun doth sweetly shine
And where the rosey buds recline
Beside the window near the seat
There sits the robin on its nest
Unstartled by the passing feet
That come and go – a happy guest
It is and all the morning long
Upon the pales it sings a song
Travel that goes afar to fare
Right happily would greet the rest
And say that comforts home was there

John Clare, from *Northborough Sonnets*

The following four lines occur in some versions of Gray's *Elegy
in a Country Churchyard*:

There scattered, oft the earliest of the year,
By hands unseen are showers of violets found;
The redbreast loves to build and warble there
And little footsteps lightly print the ground.

Thomas Gray (1716-1771)

James Grahame described robins nesting in a long and placidly descriptive section of his 'Scottish Georgics'[69].

How simply unassuming is that strain!
It is the redbreast's song, the friend of man.
High is his perch, but humble is his home,
And well concealed. Sometimes within the sound
Of heartsome mill-clack, where the spacious door,
White-dusted, tells him plenty reigns around,
Close at the root of brier-bush, that o'erhangs
The narrow stream, with shealings bedded white,
He fixes his abode, and lives at will.
Oft near some single cottage, he prefers
To rear his little home; there pert and spruce,
He shares the refuse of the goodwife's churn,
Which kindly on the wall of him she leaves:
Below her lintel of the lights, then in
He boldly flits, and fluttering loads his bill,
And to his young the yellow treasure bears.

James Grahame (1765-1811)
from *The Birds of Scotland*

The Robin's Jubilee provides, as usual, a moralistic - and anonymous - description which begins:

---

[69]   In 1828, Sophia Herbert, aged eleven, was asked to entertain her brother Charles aged ten, and her sister Fanny aged seven. So she 'sought Grahame's *Birds of Scotland*, and read of birds and their nests, and habits, and forms, till, to her great surprise, both Charles and Fanny fell asleep, even while she read of the robin and the wren.' I have quoted one short section only!

from *Contemplations on a Robin's Nest*

Thou residence of innocence and truth,
That bafflest imitation, and defiest
The studied efforts of laborious art
To form thy equal, what primeval cause
Produced thy symmetry and beauteous order?
Thou art not chance-work; a superior power
In every atom breathes; the plans divine,
Though but mere instinct framed thee as thou art...

Anonymous, from *The Robin's Jubilee* (1826)

Robert Bridges noted how even the tamest of robins becomes secretive when nesting:

Gay robin is seen no more:
        He is gone with the snow,
        For winter is o'er
        And robin will go.
In need he was fed, and now he is fled
        Away to his secret nest.
        No more will he stand
        Begging for crumbs,
        No more he comes
        Beseeching our hand
        And showing his breast
        At window and door:-
Gay robin is seen no more.

Blithe robin is heard no more:
        He gave us his song
        When summer was o'er
        And winter was long:
He sang for his bread and now he is fled

Away to his secret nest.
And there in the green
Early and late
Alone to his mate
He pipeth unseen
And swelleth his breast;
For us it is o'er:-
Blithe robin is heard no more.

Robert Bridges (1844-1930)

The next excerpt is from the lively pen of 'Forestiera' in *Kidd's Own Journal*[70], mentioned in Chapter 3.

Some very remarkable 'facts', completely establishing the amiability of the 'Hen' Robin

['She' writes a long and flowery Preface]

'Well; after this long preface to win your favour, I will at once try your good temper. *I have taken the nest of a* ROBIN, full of young ones!! Having made the confession, *my* mind is easy; let me trust *yours* is also. But,

---

[70] Kidd's stated aim was to 'gather up… certain elegant trifles that otherwise might wander down the stream of time and perish in forgetfulness.' One further extract from the journal is irresistible: 'There are two bantam hens in the possession of a lady at Plumstead, which have each laid an egg each morning for the last eighteen months, *except on Sunday*, and never once during the whole of that period has an egg been found on that day in either of their nests.' Clearly, sabbatarian principles have changed – J. Hickey, in his *Guide to Bird Watching* (1943) analysed ornithological records from New York in the 1940s and discovered that most of the spring migrants arrive on Sundays, with some on Saturday afternoons! In the present climate of professional ornithology, I fear that even that acknowledgement of Sundays may no longer be maintained.

to my little anecdote; for I feel now, my heart is yours. Early this spring, a hen robin (such a love!) between whom and myself a strict intimacy has subsisted for years, - took me into the fondest confidence as to her proposed future movements. She brought in successively moss, dry leaves, fibres of roots and horse hair; and with these, when exhibited, she flew into the garden to construct a nest. Some time subsequently, she haunted me more than ever, and took from me mealworms by the dozen. As she did not herself eat them, I guessed they were for her offspring. I was right. At this time the weather became bitterly cold – so cold, that I left her ladyship to perform her arduous duties without attempting to indulge my curiosity, - a thing you will say, in one of my sex, perfectly unaccountable! Time however, and the remorselessness of the winds, soon disclosed to me the 'local habitation' of my pet. It *had been* artfully concealed in the very spot I suspected; it was *now* patent to the passer by. Still, I forbore to remove it. Furiously raged the wind, while I was thus deliberating; and humanity decided that I was 'right' in taking that nest. Only two mornings previously, I had found two unfledged blackbirds lying dead on the ground. They had been dislodged from their nest by the wind, and they had been half-mangled, let me add, by the teeth of some daintily-fed brute of a cat, whose refined appetite, it would seem, refused to 'eat' them. I think, under *such* circumstances 'dear Mr Kidd', I shall stand acquitted in your estimation.

'The nest was secured to an ivy-branch. There were in it one unproductive egg and five young birds. Two (the finest) were lost through my cruel stupidity, from cold, the following morning. To the remaining three nestlings, I can say I have done my duty; been up with them early and late – made an indefatigable search for mealworms, though not always able to procure a sufficiency, - and digging perseveringly for insects, although from the cold dry weather (I suppose), I once only succeeded in obtaining two earwigs, and a long thin something with many legs; nor was the robin much more successful.

'Earthworms she would not give the young; nor bread and milk, nor hard yolk of egg, nor minced raw meat, nor flies, nor anything I could obtain, or think of. She showed me once a spider, at another time a caterpillar, intimating, doubtless, such would be acceptable. The rose leaves were searched, but no caterpillar rewarded my pains-taking. In spite however of our difficulties, the three young ones have left the nest, perfect beauties! They are nicely fledged, and although with nearly invisible tails, they fly, hop, chirp merrily, and eat voraciously. And now will you kindly tell me, whether I had better keep them awhile, or let them go at once? Let them fly from the window, or take the cage to the garden?'

'Forestiera'[71] in a letter to *Kidd's Own Journal* ,
5 June 1852

'Forestiera' has both greater charm and greater accuracy than Johann Eckermann, whose bird stories in *Conversations with Goethe* come over as if he needed to show how clever he was to have been close to the great man. At dinner on Monday 8 October, 1827, Eckermann tells us how in captivity a bird will sometimes adopt the young of another species:

'Last summer, in the neighbourhood of Tiefurt, I took two young wrens, which had probably only just left their nest, for they sat upon a bush on a twig with seven other young ones in a row, and the old bird was feeding them.

---

[71] 'Correspondence' continued, though it becomes clear that 'Forestiera' is Kidd's own *alter ego*!

I put the young birds in my silk pocket-handkerchief, and went towards Weimar, as far as the shooting-house; I then turned to the right towards the meadow, down along the Ilm, and passed the bathing-place, and then again to the left to the little wood. Here I thought I had a quiet spot to look once more at the wrens. But when I opened my handkerchief they both slipped out, and disappeared in the bushes and grass, so that I sought them in vain. Three days afterwards, I returned by chance to the same place, and hearing the note of a robin, guessed there was a nest in the neighbourhood, which, after looking about for some time, I really found. But how great was my astonishment, when I saw in this nest, besides some young robins nearly fledged, my two young wrens which had established themselves very comfortably, and allowed themselves to be fed by the old robins!'

' "That is one of the best ornithological stories I have ever heard", said Goethe. "I drink success to you, and good luck to your investigations. Whoever hears that, and does not believe in God, will not be aided by Moses and the prophets. That is what I call the omnipresence of the Deity, who has everywhere spread and implanted a portion of His endless love, and has intimated even in the brute as a germ, that which only blossoms to perfection in noble man!"

'While we thus conversed on good and deep matters over our dinner in the open air…'

from *Conversations of Goethe with Eckermann* (1836), translated by John Oxenford

His bird stories are of questionable truth. Goethe was an able zoologist and may have been less convinced by them than Eckermann implies.

Young robins are mistaken for young thrushes by many people as they are spotted and have no trace of red at fledging. James Grahame, in the same poem quoted earlier, describes them:

> What little birds, with frequent shrillest chirp,
> When honeysuckle flowers succeed the rose,
> The inmost thicket haunt? Their tawny breasts,
> Spotted with black, bespeak the youngling thrush,
> Though less in size; it is the redbreast's brood,
> New flown, helpless, with still the downy tufts
> Upon their heads. But soon their full-fledged wings,
> Long hesitating , quivering oft, they stretch:
> At last, encouraged by the parent voice,
> And leading flight, they reach the nearest bush,
> Or, falling short, lie panting on the ground;
> But, reassured, the destined aim attain.

James Grahame (1765-1811),
from *The Birds of Scotland*

The robin will feed on almost any insect it can get and some other invertebrates. It takes caterpillars (often seen as 'worms') especially for its young. In late Summer and autumn, it also eats small fruits. These habits have been the occasion for some of the few disparaging references to robins:

from *The Pilgrim's Progress*

'Then, as they were coming in from abroad, they espied a little robin with a great spider in his mouth; so the Interpreter said, 'Look here'. So they looked, and Mercy wondered; but Christiana said, 'What a disparagement is it to such a pretty bird as the robin-redbreast is, he being also a bird above many, that loveth to maintain a kind of sociableness with man; I had thought they had lived on crumbs of bread, or upon such other harmless matter. I like him worse than I did.'

'The Interpreter then replied, 'This robin is an emblem, very apt to set forth some Professors by; for to sight they are, as this robin, pretty of Note, Colour, and Carriage. They seem also to have a very great Love for Professors that are sincere; and above all other, to desire to sociate with them, and to be in their company, as if they could live upon the good man's crumbs. They pretend also that therefore it is that they frequent the house of the godly and the appointments of the Lord; but when they are by themselves, as the robin, they can catch and gobble up spiders, they can change their Diet, drink Iniquity, and swallow down Sin like water.' '

John Bunyan (1628-1688)

from *The History of Sandford and Merton*

'[Thomas Merton's tutor, Mr Barlow] went to the window, and desired Tommy to come to him and observe a robin which was then hopping upon the grass with something in its mouth; and asked him what he thought it was.

Tommy: I protest, sir, it is a large worm. And now he has swallowed it! I should never have thought such a pretty bird could be so cruel.

Mr Barlow: Do you imagine that the bird is conscious of all that is suffered by the insect?

Tommy: No, sir.

Mr Barlow: In him then it is not the same cruelty which it would be in you, who are endowed with reason and reflection. Nature has given him a propensity to animal food, which he obeys in the same manner as the sheep and ox when they feed upon grass, or the ass when he browses upon the furze or thistles.'

Thomas Day (1748-1789)

In Chapter 5 we saw Gilbert White's opinion of a robin's song. His further references only reinforce his dislike:

'2nd September 1774: Notwithstanding the prejudices in their favour, they do much mischief in gardens to the summer fruits.

10th September 1781: Redbreasts feed on elder-berries, enter rooms and spoil the furniture.'

Gilbert White (1720-1793), first quote from The Natural History of Selborne; second quote from The Journals of Gilbert White, ed. by W. Johnson

Tennyson, twice in the *Idylls of the King*, uses the attitude of a robin while feeding to describe Geraint looking at Enid:

And glancing all at once as keenly at her[72]
As careful robins eye the delver's toil,...

Alfred, Lord Tennyson (1809-1892)
from Idylls of the King

---

[72]   This, in Chapter 3; in Chapter 4 the line before is: 'With that he turned and looked as keenly at her'. Both times he makes her blush but for different reasons.

Dorothy Wordsworth made an observation that inspired her brother to write:

The Redbreast and the Butterfly

Art thou the bird whom man loves best,
The pious bird with the scarlet breast,
 Our little English Robin;
The bird that comes about our doors
 When autumn winds are sobbing?
Art thou th' Peter of Norway Boors?
 Their Thomas in Finland,
 And Russia far inland?
The bird, whom by some name or other
All men who know thee call their brother,
The darling of the children and men?
Could father Adam open his eyes,
And see this sight beneath the skies,
He'd wish to close them again.

If the Butterfly knew but his friend,
Hither his flight he would bend;
And find his way to me
Under the branches of the tree;
In and out, he darts about;
Can this be the bird, to man so good,
That, after their bewildering,
Did cover with leaves the children,
So painfully in the wood?

What ailed thee, Robin, that thou could'st pursue
 A beautiful creature,
 That's gentle by nature?
 Beneath the summer sky
 From flower to flower let him fly;
 'Tis all that he wishes to do.

The cheerer thou of our in–door sadness,
He is the friend of our summer gladness:
What hinders, then, that ye should be
Playmates in sunny weather,
And fly about in the air together!
His beautiful wings in crimson are drest,
A crimson as bright as thine own:
If thou would'st be happy in thy nest,
O pious Bird! whom man loves best,
Love him or leave him alone.

William Wordsworth (1770-1850)

Inexperienced robins will pick up a brightly-coloured butterfly, but careful observation has shown that they are nearly always dropped. Dorothy should have observed the bird a little longer.

The robin may well have difficulty finding sufficient food, especially in winter:

The Robin

When up aloft
I fly and fly,
I see in pools
The shining sky,
And a happy bird
Am I, am I!

When I descend
Toward the brink
I stand and look
And stop and drink
And bathe my wings,
And chink, and prink.

When winter frost
Makes earth as steel,
I search and search
But find no meal,
And most unhappy
Then I feel.

But when it lasts
And snows still fall,
I get to feel
No grief at all
For I turn to a cold, stiff
Feathery ball!

Thomas Hardy (1840-1928)

from *Winter*

In rigorous hours, when down the iron lane
The redbreast looks in vain,
For hips and haws,
Lo, shining flowers upon my window-pane
The silver pencil of the winter draws

Robert Louis Stevenson (1850-1894)

Another bit of poor observation was recorded anonymously, the only literary reference I can find to robins moulting. The moult is the one time that they do not sing:

from *Sonnet to the Redbreast*

But why now, Robin! dost thou sing so sweet!
For Time, I see, has made a peck at thee –
Bereft thee of thy tail – thou canst not see't
Or else, perhaps, thou would'st not sing so free.

Anonymous, in *European Magazine*, quoted by J. Taylor,
Tales of the Robin (1815)

A final word in this chapter about migration. It may come as a surprise to learn that one of our most obviously resident birds migrates and, indeed, most British robins do not migrate:

'It is said to be a migratory species, but from no other reason than their more frequent and numerous appearance about our habitations in winter.'

G. Montagu, from *Ornithological Dictionary* (1802)

But some do:

'Of the female robins [in South Devon] between one-third and one-quarter are non-migratory, and a few apparent migrants really move only locally; the rest migrate. Of the males most are non-migratory, but perhaps a small proportion of the first-year males and possibly a few older males migrate.'

David Lack, from *The Life of the Robin* (4th Edn,, 1965)

This means that, in winter, in many parts of Britain male robins outnumber females. They hold individual territories and at this season, the remaining females sing like the males. Further evidence for migration comes from the fact that robins can be seen on offshore islands where they do not breed, especially in autumn. Edward Rushton (Chapter 8) recorded one on a slave vessel. Sometimes they come in large numbers, such as those that greeted John Bastwick in the Isles of Scilly (Chapter 4).

Continental robins migrate much more. This led Aristotle to what seems to us the strangest conclusion that, because he saw robins only in winter and redstarts only in summer, the one species turned into the other. William Turner (1508-1568), whose observations on nests we saw earlier, refuted this ancient wisdom through simple but decisive personal observation:

'All that Aristotle has written of these two birds Pliny has copied from him into his own work. But in this matter each of them has wandered greatly from the path of truth. For both the birds are seen at the same time; moreover, tame redbreasts, when fed in cages, constantly retain the same appearance. The redbreast has a ruddy breast no less in summer than in winter. The redstart male has a black head, a red tail, but otherwise is like the female. The female redstart and its brood are so much like young redbreasts that they can scarcely be distinguished by the sharpest eye. But by the motion of the tail they may be recognised. For the redbreasts, although they move the tail, yet after they have lowered it, at once raise it again, nor does it quiver twice or thrice as does that of the redstart.'

William Turner, from *Avium Praecipuarum* …(1544), trans. A.H. Evans, as *Turner on Birds* (1903)

Turner thought that robins may simply avoid cities in summer, while redstarts are only present in summer. Actually both are migratory.

John Ruskin, in his famous lecture on robins, stated:

> 'In none of the old natural history books can I find any account of the robin as a traveller, but there is, for once, some sufficient reason for their reticence. He has a curious fancy in his manner of travelling. Of all birds, you would think he was likely to do it in the cheerfullest way, and he does it in the saddest. Do you chance to have read, in the Life of Charles Dickens, how fond he was of taking long walks in the night and alone? The robin, en voyage, is the Charles Dickens of birds.'

John Ruskin (1819-1900), from *Love's Meinie. Three Lectures on Greek and English Birds* (1873)

A few other authors have recorded migrating robins:

On a Redbreast singing at the Grave of Plato
(in the Grove of Academe)

The rose of gloaming everywhere!
And through the silence cool and sweet
A song falls through the golden air
And stays my feet –
For there! ….
This very moment surely I have heard
The sudden, swift, incalculable word
That takes me o'er the foam
Of these empurpling, dim Ionian seas,
That takes me home
To where

Far on an isle of the far Hebrides
Sits on a spray of gorse a little home-sweet bird.

The great white Attic poplars rise,
And down their tremulous stairs I hear
Light airs and delicate sighs.
Even here
Outside this grove of ancient olive-trees,
Close by this trickling murmuring stream,
Was laid long, long ago, men say,
That lordly Prince of Peace
Who loved to wander here from day to day,
Plato, who from this Academe
Sent radiant dreams sublime
Across the troubled seas of time,
Dreams that not yet are passed away,
Nor faded grown, nor grey,
But white, immortal are
As that great star
That yonder hangs above Hymettos' brow.

But now
It is not he, the Dreamer of the Dream,
That holds my thought.
Greece, Plato, and the Academe
Are all forgot:
It is as though I am unloosed by hands:
My heart aches for the grey-green seas
That hold a lonely isle
Far in the Hebrides,
An isle where all day long
The redbreast's song
Goes fluting on the wind o'er lonely sands.

So beautiful, so beautiful
Is Hellas, here.

Divinely clear
The mellow golden air,
Filled, as a rose is full,
Of delicate flame:
And oh the secret tides of thought and dream
That haunt this slow Kephisian stream!
But yet more sweet, more beautiful, more dear
The secret tides of memory and thought
That link me to the far-off shore
For which I long –
Greece, Plato, and the Academe forgot
For a robin's song!

'Fiona Macleod' (William Sharp) (1855-1905)

The next poem must take the prize as the worst doggerel written about a robin but, like William McGonagall and the Tay Bridge, it has its own charm:

from *The Redbreast of Aquitania*[73]

But there came anon,
As we journey'd on
Down the deep Garonne,
  An acquaintancy,
Which we deemed, I count,
Of more high amount,
It oped the fount
  Of sweet sympathy.

---

[73] These are verses 4-7 and 9 of 18. He prefaces it with quotes and adds a narrative beside it such as 'Not ye famous albatross of that ancient mariner olde Coleridge, but a poore robin.', and the next nine verses moralising about the death.

'Twas a stranger drest
In a downy vest,
'Twas a wee Redbreast,
   (Not an 'Albatross')
But a wanderer meek,
Who fain would seek
O'er the bosom bleak
   Of that flood to cross.

And we watched him oft
 As he soared aloft
On his pinions soft,
   Poor wee weak thing,
And we soon could mark
That he sought our bark
As a resting ark
   For his weary wing.

But the bark, fire-fed,
On her pathway sped,
And shot far ahead
   Of the tiny bird,
And quicker in the van
Her swift wheels ran,
As the quickening fan
   Of his winglets stirred.

And 'twas plain at last
He was flagging fast,
That his hour had past
   In that effort vain;
Far from either bank,
Sans a saving plank,
Slow, slow he sank,
   Nor uprose again.

'Father Prout' (Francis Sylvester Mahony) (1804-1866)

'24th February (1911) – A wild and boisterous day; ere we had traversed one-half of the intervening moorland, a blinding snow-squall drove us to the shelter of a friendly crag. Therein, quite unwittingly, we disturbed the rest of other refugees. These included both mistle and song-thrushes, skylarks, and even a robin redbreast. Thus, even so early as February, do the incipient stages of bird migration become discernible to those who have eyes to read the signs. My three companions included a lady; yet all, I feared, were a trifle dubious – inclined to doubt that such homely British birds as these, to be seen daily in their own gardens or grounds, could conceivably be travellers from afar – say from Southern Spain or even from beyond the Mediterranean Sea. Almost such doctrine seemed to approach heresy! – until by the luckiest of accidents I chanced to espy driving on snow-laden blasts, the LOST LABEL here reproduced. (Inglaterra via Pyrenees, Paris & Dover.) Then all doubts were dissolved; since obviously this scrap of flotsam was a cross-channel luggage-label that, in the stress of travel, had become detached from the personal baggage of one or other of our disturbed voyagers. A few moments' reflection, and feminine intuition, always quickest, promptly diagnosed the situation – 'After all, we ought to have remembered that no robin lives on these out-bye moors!' – Thus by fortuitous trifles are great truths revealed.'

Abel Chapman (1851-1925),
from *The Borders and Beyond*

Chapter 10
'A Robin Redbreast in a Cage'

– 'Puts all heaven in a rage.'

William Blake (1757-1827), from *Auguries of Innocence*

This practice was uncommon by Blake's time, but far from negligible. The poem below, describing what a robin may feel when caught, is more typical of people's reactions to captive robins:

> Poor robin, driven in by rain-storms wild
> To lie submissive under household hands
> With beating heart that no love understands,
> And scared eye, like a child
> Who only knows that he is all alone
> And summer's gone.

'Mrs Craik' (Dinah Maria Mulock) (1826-1887)

There was a trade in caged robins:

> 'It is a very tender bird, and therefore must have its *cage lined*.'....
>
> 'The way of taking a robin redbreast is so easy and common, that every boy knows how to take him in a pitfall.'

Nicholas Cox, from *The Gentleman's Recreation* (1676)

'The robin is a handsome bird, and well adapted for showing in an Any Other Variety class of British Birds.'

R.L. Wallace, from *British Cage Birds* (1887)

'Some people are very superstitious about these birds, and would not keep one in a cage for a fortune, supposing them to bring bad luck, but I have kept a good many without having worse luck than at other times.'

G.H. Burnett, from *British Song Birds* (19th century)

'Redbreasts are a portion of the street-sold birds [in 1851], but the catch is not large, not exceeding 3,000, with a mortality of about a third. Even this number, small as it is when compared with the numbers of other singing birds sold, is got rid of with difficulty. There is a popular feeling repugnant to the imprisonment, or coercion in any way, of 'a robin', and this no doubt has its influence in moderating the demand. The redbreast is sold, when young, both in the shops and streets for 1s., when caged and singing, sometimes for £1. These birds are considered to sing best by candle light. The street-sale is a fifth, or sometimes a quarter, all young birds, or with the rarest exceptions.'

Henry Mayhew (1812–87) in
London Labour and the London Poor[74]

---

[74]   This book has a fascinating account of the street-trade in birds at that date. This included the selling of nests (a robin's nest with five eggs cost 3d.) and 'bird-duffing', that is, painting the birds to look brighter, and in particular making the hens of certain finches look like cocks, so that they would fetch a better price.

Duchess.	Sit down;
	Discourse to me some dismal tragedy.
Cariola.	O, 'twill increase your melancholy.
Duchess.	Thou art deceived:
	To hear of greater grief would lessen mine.
	This is a prison?
Cariola.	Yes, but you shall live
	To shake this durance off.
Duchess.	Thou art a fool:
	The robin redbreast and the nightingale
	Never live long in cages.

John Webster (?1578-?1630)
from *The Duchess of Malfi*

Books on how to keep cage birds, including robins, were published with much uncritical copying between them. William Kidd, of *Kidd's Own Journal* (chapter 3) gives a thoroughly ambiguous message:

'If you would have a good songster, and a friend at the same time, procure what we characterise as a 'grey', - that is, a young robin caught soon after leaving the nest. He will then moult in his new dwelling, and get used to his fate. These young 'greys' sing sweetly, and continue in song all through the winter and early spring. Old birds are of little use in cages. They mope, very rarely sing, and are very sulky. You may purchase, if you will, three or four 'greys'. Keep them in separate cages, *and prevent them seeing each other.* They will then soon discover their vocal powers; and from among them you may select a first-rate songster.

      ……

'Above all things, court their society. Speak to them, sing to them, whistle to them, play with them; but never slight them. Then you will be in high favour, and treated to unceasing strains of indescribably harmony. At tea-time, – when the kettle sings, *they* will sing. The more merry you are, the louder their song. The sight of candles, and the Christmas log, render them half frantic with joy. Suspend your birds one above the other, and *all* your orchestra will join in. Rivalry calls forth their very best efforts.

'Our readers will now perhaps ask us, seriously, whether we *recommend* so joyous a bird as the robin to be immured in a cage. Recommend such an act of excessive impropriety! Surely not. And simply for this reason. Where there is one loving tender heart to be found, there are at least a thousand made of stone or iron. On such 'bird-keepers', our advice (kind though it be) will be thrown away. They will heed none of *our* instructions.

'A garden is the proper place to court the society of Master Bob, or a country lane. Here, in the autumn, he is in all his glory. As *our* joys decay, *his* gather strength.

William Kidd (1803–67) from *The Skylark, the Woodlark and the Robin-Redbreast: an entirely original and familiar treatise on the habits of these favourite birds; containing every needful direction for their proper management*, 1856

Caged parrots or mynahs have often been taught to 'talk'; here are some examples of caged robins doing the same:

'Besides the common sort of singing birds, the ingenious Mr Mansel had a robin redbreast that not only learnt some flageolet tunes, but spoke distinctly several short sentences.'

John Morton, from *The Natural History of Northamptonshire* (1712)

'A lady in Edinburgh possesses one who very distinctly pronounces, "How do ye do?" and several other words. Her method was, early in the morning, before giving it any food, to repeat very often what she wished it to learn.'

P. Syme, from *A Treatise on British Song-Birds* (1823)

Birds can be taught to imitate the song of another bird species. Daines Barrington, one of Gilbert White's correspondents, writes:

'… educated a young robin under a very fine nightingale; which, however, began already to be out of song, and was perfectly mute in less than a fortnight. This robin afterwards sang three parts in four *nightingale*; and the rest of his song was what the bird-catchers call *rubbish*, or no particular note whatsoever.'

Hon. Daines Barrington, from Thomas Pennant's
British Zoology, Birds (1776)

Barrington had another captive robin that sang like a 'skylark-linnet', that is, like a linnet which had been raised by a skylark and so sang like a skylark. Here is a dramatic account of another 'nightingale-robin', contributed to *the Gardener's Chronicle* about the middle of the nineteenth century:

'A gentleman informed me that a friend of his was possessed of a most wonderful bird, that he should much like me to see and hear. I went at an early day to view the prodigy. On entering the house and presenting my card, I was at once ushered into the drawing-room. I there saw two nightingale cages, suspended on the wall; one of them, with a nightingale in it, had an open front, the other had a green curtain drawn down over the front concealing the inmate. After a little discourse on the subject of ornithology, my host asked me if I should like to hear one of his nightingales sing. Of course I was all expectation. Placing me beneath the cage, and drawing up the curtain before alluded to, the bird above, at a whistle from his master, broke out in a succession of strains that I had never heard surpassed by any nightingale. They were indeed surprisingly eloquent. "What a nightingale!" ejaculated I. The rapid utterance of the bird, his perfect abandon to the inspiration of his music, and his indifference to all around him, caused me involuntarily to exclaim with Coleridge,

'– that strain again!
Full fain it would delay me.'

'And so it did. I stood riveted to the spot, knowing how seldom nightingales in a cage so deported themselves. After listening some time, and expressing my astonishment at the long-repeated efforts of the performer, so unusual, I asked to be allowed a sight of him. Permission was granted; and I saw before me – a *robin*. This bird had been brought up under the nightingale from its very earliest infancy, and not only equalled, but very far surpassed his master in song. The robin retained not one single note of his own whereby the finest ear could detect him.'

from R. Lee, *Anecdotes of the Habits and Instincts of Birds, Reptiles and Fishes* (c. 1850)

Encouraging cage birds to sing – an illustration from G.P. Olina,
Uccelliera (Manual of Birds) 1622

Poems about captive robins are rare, though there was an anonymous madrigalist:

> See, see, mine own sweet jewel
> What I have for my darling,
> A robin redbreast and a starling.
> These I give both in hope, to move thee,
> Yet thou saist that I love not, no I love not thee;
> Thou saist I do not love thee.
>
> Anonymous (1606)

The following three poems are from *The Robin's Jubilee* of 1826. The book takes its customary moral stance (although surely everyone would agree with Phillis in the first poem), and retains the anonymity of the poets:

The Robin's Nest

> Last spring, when the swallows returned back again,
> And Flora with daisies had powdered the plain,
> I ran to the maid whom my heart most approves
> To tell her of this, and that bloom decked the groves.
> The maid was directing her vine o'er the bower,
> To keep off the sun and to shield from the shower.
> Well pleased with the tidings, she made me engage
> To furnish a robin to sing in her cage.
>
> In time, O! ye shepherds! Attend to my lay,
> I ne'er can forget while there's bloom on the spray,
>
> A ram in a thicket had fastened his horn,
> And struggled and baa'd, to be quit of the thorn.
> I ran to release him, and there I admired
> A nest of those sweet ones my Phillis required.

I took from the brake the dear innocent train,
And enraptured to Phillis flew over the plain.

So soon as she saw me the boon she confessed,
And with pleasure accepted the robin's sweet nest –
How strange the transition! She looked on the young,
Her eye dropped a tear, and soft pity her tongue.
'Ah! Damon!' (she said) with a heart-piercing sigh,
'It would grieve me to death if these charmers should die –
Though great should my care be to rear up the nest,
The parent, my Damon, can cherish them best.'

I kissed her for this, and commended the maid.
That instant we ran with the nest to the shade,
As soon as we'd placed it in safety again,
The birds came delighted to cherish their train.
My Phillis approved, and with pleasure confessed
That much might be learned from the birds and their nest.
I told her through life it should be my delight
To copy the precepts displayed to my sight.
The robin, in turn, though not given to roam,
Delightfully sang all the way to our home.
On Sunday we went to the church on the hill,
Where our good aged parson exerted his skill;
And we promised each other to act for the best,
And ever remember the robin's sweet nest.

Anonymous, from *The Robin's Jubilee* (1826)

from *Lines to a Caged Robin, in a City Coffee House*

> My pretty, pretty Bob,
> Why could mankind thee rob;
> A beauteous thing like thee,
> Of darling liberty?

It prompts my deepest sigh,
To view thy speaking eye!
Look out for prison's wire:
No bush, no briar is here,
No lovely atmosphere,
In which to peck and sing,
And thoughts familiar bring

......

I'll ope thy cage – possess thee –
And liberty shall bless thee
Again my pretty Bob

Anonymous, from *The Robin's Jubilee*

The third poem is an ode which was originally '...on the Death of
Mätzel, a favourite Bullfinch', but the compiler substituted Robin
for Mätzel each time. It begins:

from *On the Death of a caged Robin*

Try not, my Stanhope, 'tis in vain
To stop your tears, to hide your pain,
Or check your honest rage;
Give sorrow and revenge their scope,
My present joy, your future hope,
  Lies murdered in his cage.

Robin's no more! Ye graces, loves,
Ye linnets, nightingales, and doves,
  Attend the untimely bier;
Let every sorrow be expressed,
Beat with your wings each mournful breast,
  And drop the natural tear.

from *The Robin's Jubilee* (1826), based on a letter from
Sir Charles H. Williams (1708-59), to Philip Stanhope, Esq.

A popular song went:

Sweet Robin

Stay, little foolish, flutt'ring thing,
Whither, ah! Whither would you wing
Your airy flight? Stay here and sing,
    The mistress to delight.

No, no sweet Robin, you shall not go;
Where, you wanton, could you be
Half so happy as with me?

Anonymous, from *The Robin Redbreast:*
A New Song Book (1828)

Despite these references, keeping caged robins or exploiting them in any way, was clearly unpopular. No doubt this was reinforced by the various folk rhymes mentioned in Chapter 6. In Cawwood the Rook (1640), Rubert the Robin suggested that nobody catches robins and:

'The raven as unfit for food… and the pretty robin redbreast for its innocency, are very seldom killed.'

Thomas Tryon, from *The Way to Health, Long Life and*
Happiness (1683)

Other European countries had a different attitude. From Germany, comes a reference first, to catching the robins and then, putting them to a curious domestic use:

'In spring, when the redbreasts frequent the hedges and bushes, sticks are passed transversely through them, on which limed twigs are fastened, then two persons gently

227

beat the hedge or bush to drive the birds towards the twigs, where they are soon caught, for redbreasts have the habit of perching on all the little low projecting branches, in order that they may discover earthworms. This sort of redbreast-chase is very common in Thuringia, where many persons keep them....

'The inhabitants of my neighbourhood like to see redbreasts hopping about the room, and they make a roost for them of oak or elm branches. They find that this bird destroys flies and even bugs.'

J.M. Bechstein (1757-1822), from *The Natural History of Cage Birds* (translated by J. Rennie)

This account is confirmed by Bechstein's contemporary, J.A. Naumann (1744-1826), in his book, *Naturgeschichte der Land - und Wasservogel*. He stated that country people would entice a robin into the living-room in autumn, and the window was then closed until the spring, so that the bird could not escape. He added fleas and cheese-mites to the list of pests that they destroyed.

As for the killing and/or eating of robins, references nearly all come from outside Britain. There is a curious reference in Ben Jonson's masque, *Love Restored*. Robin Goodfellow comes to the court, only to find that there is no masque, and exclaims:

'Would I had kept me to my gambols o' the country still, selling of fish, short service, shoeing the wild mare, or roasting of robin redbreast.'

Ben Jonson, from *Love Restored* (c. 1610)

This may refer to some custom or game of attacking a robin, probably symbolic rather than literally roasting (Chapter 6). The few English references to the eating of robins are probably copied from each other and from French sources:

> 'robin redbreasts are esteemed a light and good meat.'
>
> Thomas Mouffet, from Health's Improvement (1595), also
quoted by R. Lovell in Panzoologicomineralogia (1661)

> 'These birds are not often found in the vicinity of the kitchen, excepting as winter beggars. They are not sufficiently numerous to make a dish, although we are informed by one Hayward that the robin redbreast is remarkable for a delicate bitter flavour, for which reason it is recommended that they should be cooked and eaten like larks. [and under Larks] It is to the French cook that we are indebted for the present perfection of their cooking.' [Thirty-one recipes follow.]
>
> T.F. Garrett (ed.) Encyclopaedia of Practical Cookery
(19th century)

> 'In autumn they [robins] are very fat, and delicate food.'
>
> I. Johnson, from The Natural History of Birds … intended
for the amusement and instruction of children (1789)

In much of continental Europe, robins migrate, and it is migratory robins that are fat, as the French know, so Johnson would have found this in a French book. Most English robins do not migrate.

In Britain the robin was also used as a medicine:

> 'It is good food, and its medicinal virtues are the same with those of the sparrow, to which I refer you … The flesh of the hedge sparrow, authors say, is admirable to break the stone and expel it, being broiled and eaten with salt, or gently calcined, or burnt, dried to ashes and so taken ( ) of the said ashes or powder i, powder

of winter-cherries i, salt of tartar, sal prunellae aa gr. x mix for a dose for the same purpose, and to open all obstructions of the veins, ureters and bladder.'

W. Salmon, from *Seplasium, the Compleat English Physician of the Druggist's Shop Opened* (1693)

Such ashes, mixed with other ingredients, were also prescribed for epilepsy and other cerebral problems. A robin's dung and other ingredients were used for stomach ailments and to clear the skin of scurf, sunburn, and freckles. Some fashionable medicines of today claim to be similarly cure-all, although powder of robin is no longer an ingredient.

References from abroad, especially from the Mediterranean countries, suggest a very different picture:

'[The robin] arrives in the Levant in October, seldom passing into the open islands, but seeking the luxuriant myrtle-groves of Scio, and those other islands which offer shade and shelter. There the Greek bird-catcher takes them by dozens in the snares to which, assured by the presence of their murderer, they offer themselves.'

W.J. Broderip, from *Zoological Recreations* (1857), quoting the French traveller Sonnini

'In Italy, I remember the market-place of a picturesque town where the walls of the palaces, painted in fresco, were framed by shimmering blue hills. In the foreground, laughing girls drew water from an ancient marble fountain; figs, grapes, and peaches were profusely heaped in baskets all around them. Whilst viewing the scene, my attention was caught by a brilliant string of colour garlanding one booth to another; that string consisted of dead bullfinches, wrens, thrushes, tomtits, greenfinches; ay, also robins.'

Lady Lindsay, from *About Robins* (1889)

'At the bird-market near the rotunda in Rome, I have counted more than fifty robin redbreasts lying dead on one stall. 'Is it possible', said I to the vendor, 'that you can kill and eat these pretty songsters?' 'Yes,' said he, with a grin; 'and if you will take a dozen of them home for your dinner to-day, you will come back for two dozen tomorrow.'

Charles Waterton (1782-1865)[75],
from *Essays on Natural History, Third Series* (1857)

'Until I visited Italy, I had no conception that the redbreast existed anywhere in Europe in such abundance as to outnumber every other bird except the song-thrush and the sparrow. It is only when one has turned over piles of fresh-killed robins on the street barrows that one realises the immense numbers of the 'Pettirosso' that succumb to the guile of the professional birdcatcher.

---

[75] Waterton was a truly remarkable man. Traveller, naturalist and eccentric, he inherited Walton Hall near Wakefield, and in 1820 created a wildlife haven, effectively the first nature reserve, especially for herons, then much persecuted. An ardent Catholic, the observation quoted was made on his second visit to Rome. He records in these essays how he celebrated his first visit, in 1817: 'I fell in with my old friend and schoolfellow, Captain Jones. Many a tree we had climbed together in the last century; and, as our nerves were in excellent trim, we mounted to the top of St. Peter's, ascended the cross, and then climbed thirteen feet higher, where we reached the point of the conductor, and left our gloves on it. After this, we visited the castle of St. Angelo, and contrived to get on the head of the guardian angel, where we stood on one leg.' Waterton's second visit was made about twenty years later; he merely walked in bare-footed.

'Di Valli instructs us that the Roman plan of catching the 'Pettirosso' is to employ a tame robin as a decoy. This is placed in a spherical cage mounted on a spiked staff, so that it can be easily planted in the ground. A number of limed twigs are grouped around the cage of the decoy, to which Savi gives the name of the 'Gaggia'. The peasant carries his decoy to some copse in which he expects to find a robin. He then challenges the wild bird with a bird-whistle, or with the 'Chioccolo'. The pugnacious 'Pettirosso' flies in a fury to the fray, but while endeavouring to attack his caged rival is himself held fast by the limed twigs. Robins are caught in the 'Brescianella', in trap-cages, snares, and in many other ways. But the chief market supply is obtained by the instrumentality of the 'Civetta' or Little Owl. The fowler leaves home as soon as the dew has dried on the grass, and marches along the hedgerows until he hears the sweet cadence of the redbreast's strain. The 'Civetta' is then placed on the perch ('Gruccia'), which is always employed for the Little Owl. The specimen of this perch which I brought from Italy consists of two parts, the staff and the circular headpiece. This latter is covered with cloth, above which a loose network is spread, to give the owl a firm seat. The staff on which the headpiece revolves (for it is not fixed, but can be spun round at pleasure) consists of a piece of hard wood fitted with an iron spike at the extremity.

The 'Civetta' is allowed to hop to the end of the leash attached to the swivel which secures it to the jesses of the bird. The fowler places the 'Civetta' in an open space, and arranges a few limed twigs ('Panioni') about the nearest bushes, or above the turf, in the likeliest positions for the wild 'Pettirosso' to alight. The fowler then hides behind a hedge to watch the effect of the owl upon the redbreast. The little bird soon emerges from the shadow of the hedge, and hops from one place

The 'Civetta' from G.P. Olina, *Uccelliera* (Manual of Birds) 1622

233

to another in the hopes of securing a better view of the "Civetta" At last he perches on one of the limed rods, when his curiosity seals his fate. If the fowler finds that the first redbreast which he wishes to take proves too crafty to succumb to his wiles, he takes his owl up and moves on to some more auspicious spot. A clever fowler has been known to capture one hundred and fifty or even two hundred robins in a single day with the aid of a 'Civetta'.'

Rev. H.A. MacPherson,
from *A History of Fowling* (1897)

'No bird is earlier awake than the redbreast; it begins the music of the woods, welcomes the dawn of day. It also protracts its warble to the latest hour, and is seen fluttering about in the evening. It is often caught in gins after there is scarce light sufficient for taking it up. It has little shyness: and its volatility, its restlessness, or its curiosity, hurry it into every sort of snare. It is always the first bird that is caught by the decoy; even the voice of the fowlers, and the noise made in cutting the branches, attract it; and it alights behind them, and is entangled by the springe or limed twig, the instant they are set. It answers equally the scream of the brown owl, or the sound of the slit leaf of ivy. Their feeble cry *uîp, uîp,* whistled on the finger, or the chirping of some other bird, is sufficient to put all the redbreasts round in motion. They fly to the spot, sounding from a distance *tirit, tiritit, tirititit,* with a sonorous ringing which is not their modulated air, but what they chirp in the morning and evening, and whenever they are excited by a new object. They brush eagerly through the whole of the call-ground, till they are stopped by some of the limed twigs, which are placed in the avenues, or fastened to poles that are made low on purpose to intercept their flight, which is seldom more than four or five feet from the surface; if one disentangles itself, it makes a third small cry *tí-í, tí-í,* which alarms the rest, and stops their further approach. They may also be caught in the open parts of the woods by means of poles, to which are fastened nooses and limed twigs; but the springes are the most sure and successful; now is it requisite that these be baited; we need only set them in the edge of glades, or in the middle of paths, and the unfortunate little bird, pushed on by curiosity, will throw itself into the snare.'

G. Buffon (1707-1788)
from *Histoire Naturelle des Oiseaux,*
trans. by W. Smellie (1791)

In 1916 another French writer, A. Godard, estimated that, in the district of Le Var alone, around Toulon, twenty thousand robins were destroyed in one season. A world-famous French zoologist included in his text-book that:

'the redbreasts are more numerous in Lorraine and Burgundy than elsewhere. They are very much sought after there, and their flesh acquires an excellent fat, which renders it a very delicate meat.'

Baron G. Cuvier (1769-1832), from
La Regne Animal (1817)

Other travellers give accounts of robins for sale in countries around the Mediterranean and it was common in Germany, until prohibited by law, in the nineteenth century. At the end of the eighteenth century, J.A. Naumann (1744-1826) noted that the country people killed robins for food in large numbers, threading their bodies together for sale in the market (from *Naturgeschichte der Land – und Wasservogel*).

There is no doubt that robins are still persecuted in Mediterranean Europe and North Africa, but EU legislation from 1979 has curtailed it considerably. The great displays of robins in French and Italian markets are, thankfully, past.

At the end of the nineteenth century we find that robins were killed for other ends:

> 'of late years an additional impulse has been given to the capture of this species by the absurd fashion of using its skin for the trimming of ladies' dresses.'
>
> A. Newton, from *A Dictionary of Birds* (1893-6)

> 'It is fervently to be hoped that, in time, ladies will altogether give up the habit of wearing these little birds stuffed, on their hats and gowns. For my own part, I would as lief wear a stuffed village child, or, what to many would seem more horrible, a carefully-prepared defunct pug-dog.'
>
> Lady Lindsay, from *About Robins* (1889)

The fashion for robin skins clearly did not last, for the Royal Society for the Protection of Birds, founded in 1889, has no record of it.

There is one other Victorian slaughter of robins, this time in the famous Crystal Palace, just after being moved to Sydenham, from Hyde Park, in 1854[76]. William Kidd protested about it, first in his *London Journal*, and later:

---

[76] This incident recalls another when the Crystal Palace was first erected in Hyde Park in 1851. Then sparrows got in and multiplied, causing the queen to confront the then venerable Duke of Wellington for a solution. He allegedly suggested 'Try sparrowhawks, Ma'am', although this story only appears in print in 1931, in P. Guedalla's *The Duke*.

'We were much gratified last year, while visiting the Sydenham Palace, to observe the large number of robins (all so tame!) that had taken up their quarters in the building. So completely were they 'at home' that here they nested – introducing themselves and their young families at the dinner-table, and going through a whole round of diverting tricks to the infinite amusement of lookers-on. And how sweetly melodious were their united voices within those twelve acres of glass! Were ever such strains heard before under similar circumstances? Never! The little performers positively sang the visitors in, and *out* – trotting along the floors to the very last. It was a charming sight. Their nests were built in those very pretty wire flower-baskets, so tastefully suspended round the galleries, and made by Richards and Co., 370 Oxford Street.

'We went again this season, to get a peep at our little friends. We listened for them eagerly; we sought for them carefully. We imitated their song. Alas – no response! All was cruelly silent. Addressing ourselves to a young lady, who we rightly guessed was a season-ticket holder, we explained to her the cause of our solicitude, which had not escaped her observation. "Oh – sir!" sighed this fair daughter of Eve, with a seraphic expression of countenance yet visible to our mind's eye – "those dear robins, sir, have all been *poisoned*!" We groaned. On further enquiry, we found it was too true. They had been voted 'a nuisance!' – and poisoned! Who, after this shall deny that Man is a Savage?'

William Kidd, from *The Skylark, the Woodlark and the Robin-Redbreast* (1856)

In the last few years, there has been a similar story with a happier ending. Robins have found their way into our twenty-first century 'Crystal Palace'- the great glasshouses of the Eden Project in Cornwall. They have evidently enjoyed their new home. They have been delighting visitors with their singing and have been breeding inside the domes. I have not heard of any plans to poison them.

Chapter 11

Robins and Children

The first publications for children were poor quality chap-books (Chapter 2). The robin was present from the beginning, with *Who killed Cock Robin?* and *The Children in the Wood*. Then in the second half of the eighteenth century, appealing books began to be produced for children, pioneered by the publisher John Newbery. In 1786, Mrs Sarah Trimmer (1741-1810) published her *Fabulous Histories designed for the Instruction of young Children respecting their Treatment of Animals*.

Mrs Trimmer was worried by the fairy tales that were being read to children: by the magic and the lack of moral instruction. She described her book as a fable. It was an immediate favourite and was frequently re-published throughout the nineteenth century. An edition of 1815, illustrated by Thomas Bewick, was described as the 'tenth', but there were many unauthorised editions, too. It remained the most popular of all children's books until the arrival of *Alice in Wonderland* in 1865.

The heroes of the story are the redbreast children, Robin, Dicky, Flapsy and Pecksy, together with the Benson children, Harriet and Frederick. An edition of 1831 gave her book the alternative title, *The History of the Robins*, and this is how it has been known ever since. Robins were an obvious choice – small and confiding, though often slightly uncertain in human company, they have some of the same attributes as children themselves[77].

By 1845, the tale had already been twice translated into German. In the 1870s, there were two elaborate English editions, one illustrated by Harrison Weir, the other, by Giacomelli, and the first shortened and simplified versions. These later became popular in Britain and America. The book even had the distinction, perhaps unique, of being translated into words of one syllable, by the Rev. Chas. Swete, D.D., in

---

[77]   This is so prevalent that it can come as a shock when they behave like birds, for instance, when feeding on 'worms' (see Chapter 8), or migrating.

1871, except for a few proper names and the unavoidable 'red-breast', which he hyphenated. Various illustrated editions showed the Benson children in a succession of period costumes (p.248).

In one form or another, *The History of the Robins* was probably read to most of the great figures of Victorian England. It was evidently a favourite with the Queen herself, as Prince Waldemar received a copy of the Harrison Weir edition, inscribed: 'given to Waldemar by his dear Grandmamma of England, Xmas 1874.'

Mrs Yonge records reading it to her daughter Charlotte and, much earlier, Mary Shelley had the nickname of 'Pecksy', as well as 'Dormouse' and 'Maie'. She herself quotes her husband's lines about her in a flirtatious letter to Jefferson Hogg, while describing herself as a free spirit:

> On her hind paws the Dormouse stood
> In a wild and mingled mood
> Of Maieishness and Pecksietude.

Percy Bysshe Shelley (1792-1822)

Pecksy, according to Mrs Trimmer, 'was of so amiable a disposition, that it was her constant study to act with propriety, and avoid giving offence'.

The spirit in which Mrs Trimmer wrote her book is shown by an entry in her private journal for 22 September 1785: her aim was 'to do honour to my Creator, and inspire persons with right sentiments'.

The History of the Robins offered children a story with a moral, but one that they could enjoy. It was simply but beautifully written, and it included not only descriptions of country life, with delightful digressions, but also, with sound common sense. My father, in the 1930s, was teaching at Dartington Hall school and at bedtime, he read the book to the offspring of left-wing liberals, to whom moral instruction was most unfashionable! The children loved it, but then so had their spiritual ancestor, young Mary Godwin (later, Shelley). The book begins:

'In a hole, which time had made in a wall covered with ivy, a pair of redbreasts built their nest. No place could have been better chosen for the purpose; it was sheltered from the rain, screened from the wind, and in an orchard belonging to a gentleman, who had strictly charged his domestics not to destroy the labours of those little songsters which chose his ground as an asylum.

'In this happy retreat, which no idle schoolboy dared to enter the hen redbreast deposited four eggs, and then took her seat upon them, resolving that nothing should tempt her to leave the nest till she had hatched her infant brood. Her tender mate every morning brought her food, before he tasted any himself, and then cheered her with a song.

Illustrated initial letter from Sarah Trimmer's *History of the Robins,* edition of c.1879

'At length the day arrived when the happy mother heard the chirping of her little ones, pleasing to her ears, as the prattle of a beloved child to its fond parent. With inexpressible tenderness, she spread her maternal wings to cover them, threw out the egg-shells in which they before lay confined, then pressed them to her bosom, and presented them to her mate, who viewed them with rapture, and seated himself by her side that he might share her pleasure.

' "We may promise ourselves much delight in rearing our little family," said he, "but it will occasion us a great deal of trouble. I would willingly bear the whole fatigue myself, but it will be impossible for me, with my utmost labour and industry, to supply all our nestlings with what is sufficient for their daily support; it will therefore be necessary for you to leave the nest occasionally, in order sometimes to seek provisions for them." She declared her readiness to take a flight whenever it should be requisite, and said that there would be no necessity for her to be long absent, as she had in her last excursion discovered a place near the orchard where food was scattered on purpose for such birds as would take the pains of seeking it, and had been informed by a chaffinch that there was no kind of danger in picking it up. "This is a lucky discovery indeed," replied he, "and we must avail ourselves of it, for this great increase of family renders it prudent to make use of every expedient for supplying our necessities. I myself must take a larger circuit, for some insects that are proper for the nestlings cannot be found in all places; however, I will bear you company whenever it is in my power." The little ones now began to feel the sensation of hunger and opened their gaping mouths for food, on which their kind father instantly flew forth to seek it for them, and in turns supplied them all, as well as his beloved mate. This was a hard day's work, and when evening came on, he was glad to seek repose. Therefore, turning his head under his wing, he soon fell asleep. His mate followed his example. The four little ones had before fallen into a gentle slumber, and perfect quietness for some hours reigned in the nest.

'The next morning they were awakened at the dawn of day by the song of a skylark, who had a nest near the orchard; and as the young redbreasts were clamorous for food, their father cheerfully prepared himself to renew his toil, but first requested his mate to accompany him to the place she had mentioned. "That I will do," replied she, "at a proper hour, but it is too early yet; I must therefore entreat that you will go by yourself and procure a breakfast for us, as I am fearful of leaving the nestlings before the air is warmer, lest they should be chilled." To this he readily consented, and fed all his little darlings, to whom, for the sake of distinction, I shall give the names of Robin, Dicky, Flapsy, and Pecksy. When this kind office was performed, he perched on an adjacent tree and there, while he rested, entertained his family with his melody, till his mate springing from the nest called on him to attend her; on which he instantly took wing, and followed her to a courtyard belonging to an elegant mansion.

'No sooner did they appear before the parlour window, than it was hastily thrown up by Miss Harriet Benson, a little girl about eleven years old, the daughter of the Gentleman and Lady to whom the house belonged.

'Miss Harriet, with great delight, called her brother to see two robin redbreasts. Her summons was instantly complied with, and she was joined by Master Frederick, a fine, chubby, rosy-cheeked boy, about six years of age, who, as soon as he had taken a peep at the feathered strangers, ran to his mamma and entreated her to give him something to feed the birds with. "I must have a great piece of bread this morning," said he, "for there are all the sparrows and chaffinches that come every day, and two robin redbreasts besides." "Here is a piece for you, Frederick," replied Mrs Benson, cutting a roll that was on the table; "but if your daily pensioners continue to increase, as they have done lately, we must provide some other food for them, as it is not right to cut pieces from a loaf on purpose for birds, because there are many children that want bread, to whom we should give the preference. Would you deprive a poor little hungry boy of his breakfast to give it to birds?" "No," said Frederick, "I would sooner give my own breakfast to a poor boy than he should go without. But where shall I get victuals enough for my birds? I will beg the cook to save all the crumbs in the bread-pan, and those which are scattered on the table-cloth." "A very good scheme," said Mrs Benson, "and I advise you, my dear, to put it in execution; for I make no doubt it will answer your purpose if you can prevail on the servants to indulge you. I cannot bear to see the least fragment of food wasted which may conduce to the support of life in any creature."

'Miss Harriet, being quite impatient to exercise her benevolence, requested her brother to remember that the poor birds, for whom he had been a successful solicitor would soon fly away if he did not make haste to feed them; on which, he ran to the window with his treasure in his hand.'

Mrs Sarah Trimmer (1741-1810),
from *The History of the Robins*

In an episode about a 'learned pig'[78], young Harriet is gently told off by her mother for wishing to be seen and not heard. The moral, though, does become absurd in one renowned footnote, through regard for accuracy. The young robins, taken by their parents on a tour of the garden, were highly amused by a mocking-bird, until their parents pointed out that it was wrong to ridicule others by mimicry. The footnote reads: 'A mock-bird is properly a native of America, but is introduced here for the sake of the moral'.

---

[78] This 'learned pig' was also commented on by Samuel Johnson and Lord Macaulay: 'I have', said a lady who was present, 'been for a long time accustomed to consider animals as mere machines, actuated by the unerring hand of Providence to do those things which are necessary for the preservation of themselves and their offspring; but the sight of the learned pig, which has lately been shown in London, has deranged these ideas, and I know not what to think.' [The pig could evidently spell and tell the time when with his keeper and Harriet asks about it in detail. Her mother is insistent that this is 'laudable curiosity' and not at all impertinent.]

Sarah Trimmer was a remarkable person. She married and raised a family but was always concerned with the education of the poor. She wrote several books, edited more, mostly of a religious nature, and critically reviewed the books written for children. To a modern sensibility, it is odd that so many children's stories of the time included death. Death was always seen as a lesser disaster than sin, and it is well to be reminded that the fires of hell were much more real then, and a lot of children died[79]. Many stories emphasised punishment for straying from the moral line. Mrs Trimmer was heavily critical of this stance. One of the books she condemned was by 'Mr Pratt'. She stated:

> 'The story is, in our opinion, exceptionable as it now stands… "an eye for an eye, a tooth for a tooth" is not the doctrine of Christianity, even in respect for animals.'
>
> Sarah Trimmer, from her own journal, *The Guardian of Education* (1802)

She suggested that the father should have given the children a good whipping, instead of what actually happened:

The Robin

[The story begins with a description of a shepherd, his spinner wife and their numerous family. As he was too poor to give his children a good education, he gave them instruction himself on how to treat animals with respect, ending his instruction '…wanton cruelty will always be returned upon the tormentor'.]

'… it would have been well for them if they had always obeyed the precepts of their father. But now comes the cream of the story, pray therefore attend.

---

[79] One chap-book was the 'dreadful tale' of a boy who evaded Sunday school in order to slide on the ice, and fell through. As his dripping corpse was laid at the parental door, the tale concludes: 'What a sight for his afflicted parents. What a scene for a Sunday afternoon.'

'The eldest son had one day taken the nest of a robin, which consisted of five young ones, and a sixth just bursting from the shell. He carried them home to his brothers and sisters, to each of which he gave a bird; but the little nestling he gave to one of the children in the lap, who wrapping it up in a piece of flannel, put it in a small wicker basket, and set it by the fire. The boy that found the nest, tied a string to the leg of his bird, and cruelly dragged it after him. The second son ran pins through the eyes of his bird, and took a delight in seeing it bleed to death. The third gave his to the cat, or rather *pretended* to give it, for he held it first pretty close to puss's whiskers, and then pulled it away from her, but at last she pounced upon it, and carried off one of the legs. The eldest daughter intended to have taken care of hers, but one of her brothers having murdered his own, seized upon her property, and both pulling the poor wretch different ways, betwixt compassion and cruelty, it died in the contest. And the younger girl, now in possession of the only bird that was left, put hers into a cage, and covered it over with wool. At this crisis the mother, who had been gleaning, and the poor old shepherd, returned home. The limbs of the dead birds were seen upon the floor, and the cat was busily employed in a corner, at clearing them away.

'The old man insisted upon the truth. The trembling boy confessed it. "Barbarous wretches!" cried the shepherd, "is this the return for my care and instruction? But I will punish you for it." The eldest son he tied by the leg, and did to him as he did to the bird; the second son he scratched with pins, till his hands were all over blood; at the third he set his dog, who caught him by the leg as he used to catch the sheep; the eldest daughter who had lost her bird, he pitied. He kissed the second daughter, which had put her poor thing into the cage; but *hugged to his very heart* the little creature that had placed the nestling in a warm basket.

246

'Now it pleased God, that about six or seven months after this, the eldest son (which had been the cause of all this mischief) fell sick and died; and many people are now living who say, that as he was going to be put into the ground, the ravens, rooks, kites, and other vast birds, all flew over his coffin, screamed, and could by no means be got away, nor could he rest in his grave for them, because the animals were always digging up the earth under where he lay, as if they were resolved to eat him up – and some declare *he is actually gone*. I beg pardon, schoolfellows, for this long story, but I shall finish directly. I cannot help mentioning to you the different fate of the good little girl who treated the animal tenderly. A year after the death of her brother, she died herself of the smallpox, and I do assure you, it has been told to me as fact, that her grave is a perfect garden, for the robins do not suffer a single weed to grow upon it, and God Almighty has adorned it with wild flowers, as innocent as the baby which they cover.'

from *Pity's Gift, A Collection of interesting Tales to excite the Compassion of Youth for the Animal Creation*, from the Writings of Mr Pratt, selected by a Lady (1798)

Harriet And Frederick looking at the nest, from an 1833 edition of
Saraah Trimmer's *History of the Robins*

Nature books were being written for children in this period, too, again,
always with a moral flavour. Their mixture of piety, didacticism, and
kindness tells us more about the period than any political history.

> 'This work is dedicated to those good and humane
> children, who are satisfied with the contemplation of the
> beauties of nature, and who never disgrace themselves
> by robbing birds, some of its most interesting objects, of
> their eggs or their young: a practice which is as much a
> proof of a bad heart, as the forebearance and reprobation
> of it are proofs of an amiable disposition.'

from Anonymous, *History of British Birds* (1807)

248

' "But, Papa, we have not noticed any birds lately: I suppose it is because they have all done singing". "Not all, Edward; but most of them. See, perched on the topmost bough of that ash, the robin - motacilla rubecula – or redbreast, pours forth his sweet strain; to tell you, Edward, that all the birds have not done singing. He belongs to the order passeres, the same as the redstart and nightingale." '

Rev. B. H. Draper, from *The Juvenile Naturalist or Walks in the Country* (1839)

[A child tells his tame robin that he should not eat worms alive, but] 'be glad of some crumbs, instead of those crawling things: and then the cruelty, only think of that, Robin! You don't mean to be cruel, I know, any more than we do who suffer the dear little lambs and sheep to be killed that we may eat them.'

Jane Bragg, in *Birds and Insects* (1844)

Many of the writers were anonymous or describe themselves as 'A Clergyman's Wife', or as the author of some previous work. They were not interested in fame or money. We may smile at them, but they would rightly have been shocked by many of the children's books produced since, mainly for commercial gain. Of course there have been some outstandingly good books written for children ever since this time and the modern child has a huge library. *The History of the Robins* will probably not be there, but Sarah Trimmer was the pioneer.

In 1804, there appeared Mrs Charlotte Smith's *Conversations, introducing Poetry; chiefly on subjects of Natural History.* These are again moral, but simply written and, this time, were commended by Mrs Trimmer. In the fifth conversation, after remarks on God's Providence and the greenness of grass, the children's aunt (Mrs Dorset) writes to them about a tame robin:

The Robin's Petition

'A suppliant to your window comes,
Who trusts your faith, and fears no guile,
He claims admittance for your crumbs,
And reads his passport in your smile,

'For cold and cheerless is the day,
And he has sought the hedges round;
No berry hangs upon the spray,
Nor worm, nor ant-egg can be found.

'Secure his suit will be preferred,
No fear his slender feet deter;
For sacred is the household bird,
That wears the scarlet stomacher.'[80]

Lucy the prayer assenting heard,
The feathered suppliant flew to her,
And fondly cherished was the bird
That wears the scarlet stomacher.

Emboldened then, he'd fearless perch
Her netting or her work among,
For crumbs among her drawings search,
And add his music to her song;

And warbling on her snowy arm,
Or half entangled in her hair,
Seemed conscious of the double charm
Of freedom and protection there.

A graver moralist, who used
From all some lesson to infer,

---

[80] She acknowledges John Donne for this phrase (see page 95)

Thus said, as on the bird she mused,
Pluming his scarlet stomacher:

'Where are his companions now,
Who sung so merrily in spring?
Some shivering on the leafless bough,
With ruffled plume, and drooping wing.

'Some in the hollow of a cave,
Consigned to temporary death;
And some beneath the sluggish wave
Await reviving nature's breath.

'The migrant tribes are fled away,
To skies where insect myriads swarm;
They vanish with the summer day,
Nor bide the bitter northern storm.

'But still is this sweet minstrel heard,
While lours December dark and drear,
The social, cheerful, household bird,
That wears the scarlet stomacher.

'And thus in life's propitious hour,
Approving flatterers round us sport,
But if the faithless prospect lour,
They the more happy fly to court.

'Then let us to the selfish herd
Of fortune's parasites prefer
The friend like this, our winter bird,
That wears the scarlet stomacher.'

Mrs Catherine Anne Dorset (c. 1750-1817) for her
sister Mrs Charlotte Smith (1749-1806), from *Conversations,
introducing Poetry; chiefly on subjects of Natural History*

The conversation is then led to an autumn flower that can catch insects, and so to the Venus fly-trap and remarks on heathen mythology, which young Emily thought so wicked that she would not at first listen. Emily complains of the hot weather, but is rebuked for murmuring against the revolution of the seasons. The harvesting of corn is described, and then that of grapes and olives in France, a poem is added on the close of summer, which evokes questions. 'And now you may amuse yourselves for an hour or two,' the mother concludes.

In 1804, the first volume of *Original Poems for Infant Minds*, by 'several young persons' was published. Instantly popular, these verses changed the whole style of poetry for children. They were mainly written by the Taylor sisters, Jane and Ann, aged only 21 and 22 at the time, and include one of the best known of all nursery rhymes: 'Twinkle, twinkle little star'. Their simple direct style was later much imitated, usually badly:

The Robin

Away, pretty robin, fly home to your nest,
To make you my captive would please me the best,
    And feed you with worms and with bread;
Your eyes are so sparkling, your feathers so soft,
Your little wings flutter so pretty aloft,
    And your breast is all coloured with red.

But then, 'twould be cruel to keep you, I know,
So stretch out your wings, little robin, and go,
    Fly home to your young ones again;
Go listen again to the notes of your mate,
And enjoy the green shade of your lonely retreat,
    Secure from the wind and the rain.

But when the leaves fall, and the winter winds blow,
And the green fields are covered all over with snow,

And the clouds in white feathers descend;
When the springs are all ice, and the rivulets freeze,
And the long shining icicles drop from the trees,
   Then, robin, remember your friend.

If with cold and with hunger quite perished and weak
Come tap at my window again with your beak,
   And gladly I'll let you come in:
You shall fly to my bosom, or perch on my thumbs,
Or hop round the table and pick up the crumbs,
   And never be hungry again.

Jane Taylor (1783-1824)

In 1818, another famous, fiercely evangelical writer for children, Mrs
Mary Sherwood (1775-1851), wrote her *History of the Fairchild Family*.
When these children quarrelled, Mr Fairchild whipped them, and then
led them through a gloomy wood to a gibbet, where he forced them
to gaze at the face of a man who had long hung in chains for the
murder of his brother. After this, in 1820, she wrote this story about
a robin's nest that is almost a parody of the didactic style:

The Robin's Nest

'I shall never forget the uneasiness I endured when a
little girl, on account of some young robins, which I
took from their nest, with the intention of bringing
them up by hand. I well remember the day I found the
robin's nest. I had been unusually diligent in learning
my lessons and performing my tasks of work that day,
which I completed much sooner than my sisters, and so
much to mamma's satisfaction, that she allowed me to
go out and play, or amuse myself in the garden.

[She sets out on a bright spring day, describing the flowers, bees, and so on, and without a care in the world.]

'I discovered, just within the bank of an old dry mossy ditch, a robin's nest, in which were five pretty speckled birds, full fledged. Without pausing to reflect on the impossibility of providing suitable nourishment for these little birds, I resolved to make myself mistress of them. "They shall be my tame robins!" I said exulting to myself, as I deposited them, one by one, in my pinafore, and hastened homeward rejoicing in my good fortune, as I then thought it, and eager to display my prize to my sisters.

'As I opened the garden wicket, I was accosted by the gardener's son, Jonathan, who asked me if I had been gathering flowers. I briefly told him of my capture of the little robins; but instead of congratulating me, he earnestly implored me to carry the young birds back again to the nest, assuring me, that to take a robin's or wren's, or a swallow's nest, was a very wicked thing, and some misfortune was sure to happen to those that did. I told him I did not mean to hurt or kill the young robins, but to feed and cherish them, till they grew fine birds, and were as tame and handsome as the garden robins that sung so prettily; but Jonathan only shook his head, and said: "Ah, Miss Kate, you will never have any luck, depend upon it, till you take them back to the old ones." I was incredulous, and obstinately bent on trying to rear the young birds; so I left Jonathan to indulge his old-fashioned notions, and ran home as fast as I could.

'Now I must tell you that I was totally unacquainted with the nature of these birds; and was not at that time aware that their chief food, especially when young, consisted of worms, caterpillars, and a variety of other insects.

254

I brought them fruit, corn, and crumbs of bread, and whatever I thought likely to tempt them to eat; but though they were fine birds, and quite fledged, they seemed to have no notion of pecking the food I scattered before them; or they required nourishment of a different nature to that which I offered them: be it as it may, they obstinately refused all my invitations to eat or drink; and with feelings of great uneasiness I perceived first one, then another of the members of my adopted family, begin to flag. Before night came, two out of the five were in a dying condition, and a third sat at the bottom of the basket in which I had placed it, with its wings drooping, its feathers ruffled, and its eyes dim and filmy. I was too late to replace the robins that night; but I began to think I had better have followed the advice of the gardener's son. I regarded the dying robins with eyes swimming in tears, and went to bed with the determination of restoring the remaining ones to their nest as soon as possible; but, alas! when I hastened to look at my poor little captives, I found only one out of the five remained alive. He was yet lively and strong, and possibly had been induced by hunger to pick a few of the crumbs with which I had so profusely supplied the basket previous to retiring to rest. Without further hesitation I resolved on carrying the poor little bird back to his former happy home in the mossy bank, nothing doubting but that his parents would gladly receive their lost, and, no doubt, lamented nestling. With this determination, I tied on my bonnet, and carefully depositing the poor little robin in my bosom, I took my way through the shaded avenue to the meadow, through which my nearest path lay, to gain the little pasture where the robin's nest was situated. But scarcely had I reached the white gate that led to the meadow, when I was alarmed by the noisy outcries of the geese and a great white gander. These ill-natured creatures all ran forward at my approach, flapping their wings and stretching out their long necks, screaming and hissing like so many serpents.

'I must confess, at that time I was a sad cowardly child, and never had mustered courage sufficient to pass these geese, when unprotected by the presence of the nursemaid or Jonathan, the gardener's son; instead, therefore, of boldly turning about and facing them, I stood trembling on the outside of the gate, and weeping bitterly; my tears flowed from a double cause – from fear of the geese, if I went forward, and grief for the inevitable fate of the poor little bird if I went back. In sad perplexity I looked round on every side, in the vain hope of seeing someone who might protect me from my clamorous enemies (but, alas for poor little Katie! nobody appeared within sight).

'Compassion, which was heightened by a feeling of remorse for having removed the robin from the fostering care of its tender parents, which were, perhaps, even then lamenting the untimely loss of their beloved nestling, overcame my terrors, and urged me to pass the flock of geese, which had removed to a little distance, and were now quietly feeding on the grass; and, for a wonder, suffered me to pass by unmolested.

'Breathless with speed and agitation, I at length regained the avenue; having replaced the robin in its nest, I had imagined in so doing I had at least preserved him from the fate of his brother and sisters; but I was mistaken: the following day I went to visit the nest, and found the poor forsaken bird stretched on the ground beside it, stiff and cold. The parent birds had, in all probability, never returned again to the nest, after they discovered the loss of their infant brood; and the poor innocent robin was starved to death.

'This circumstance made so strong an impression on my mind, that I never from that day attempted to bring up young birds; and though I found many nests in the garden, I never touched any of the young birds, or robbed the old ones of their eggs, contenting myself with watching their parental employment, from the time of building and setting to that of hatching and feeding the callow broods: indeed, so far from molesting these innocent creatures, I became their best friend, and protected them with jealous care from those who would have taken their eggs or destroyed their young ones.'

[Another twenty pages follow on various birds' nests, and then an account of a tame robin, taken from contemporary works of natural history.]

from *Sketches from nature or Hints to Juvenile Naturalists,*
by the Author of *The Young Emigrants, The Step-Brothers, Prejudice
Reproved, Juvenile Forget Me Not, Nursery Fables, &c.,* Mrs Mary
Martha Sherwood (1775–1851)

The last robin story in the moral tradition is gentler:

Daily Bread

'Your heavenly Father knoweth that ye have need of all these things.'

Matthew, vi. 32

[The story starts with the robin singing his autumn song. The tortoise complains that it is not the time to be so cheerful with winter coming, and anyway he is trying to sleep. The robin remains determinedly cheerful, and they argue. Then, as Christmas approaches the weather turns dark and cold with snow]:

'Heavily, heavily, heavily, it came down. The robin flew about in distress, and in doing so caught sight of a heap of holly, laid aside to be carried up to the house to decorate its walls. He picked two or three of the berries from them as they lay there, and then came the gardener by, who carried the whole away. He flew after the man as he walked, and never left him until he disappeared with his load into the house. Its unfriendly doors closed against the little wanderer, and no one within knew of the wistful eyes which had watched the coveted food out of sight.

' "I have eaten; let me be thankful," was the robin's resolute remark, as he flew away from the house and returned to the holly tree, which had so lately been his storehouse of hope, and from its now stripped and barren branches, poured out, as before, his lay of glad thanksgiving for what he had had.

'Homeward from his day's work of business there passed by, at that moment, the owner and inhabitant of the little suburban villa. It had been a melancholy day to him, for it was saddened by painful recollections. It was the anniversary of the day on which his wife had been laid in the church-yard grave, and since that event two sons had sailed for the far-off land of promise, which puts a hemisphere between the loved and loving on earth. So that far-distant land held them, whilst one not so distant, perhaps, but more unattainable for the present – held the other. No wonder, therefore, that on that owner's face, as he approached his home, there hung a cloud of suffering and care, which not even the thought of the Christmas-day at hand and the children yet spared to his hearth could prevent or dispel. Verily the autumn of man's life comes down upon him as the autumn season descends upon the earth. Clouds and tears mix with whatever brightness may remain.

'All at once, however, the abstracted look of sorrow is startled. What is it that he hears? He pauses, – he stops, – he lifts up those troubled eyes. Beautiful, tender, affecting, as the voice of the cuckoo in spring, there swept over the listener's heart the autumnal song of the robin. Sing on, sing on, from the top of your desolate tree, oh little bird of cheerfulness and hope! Pour out again that heaven-taught music of contentment with the hour that now is. Shalt *thou* be confident of protection, and a *man* destitute of hope! Shalt *thou* in the depth of thy winter's trial, have joy and peace, and *man* never look beyond the cloud?

'Poor little innocent bird, he sang his pretty song to an end, and then he flew away. Quarrel not with him if, in painful recollection of the holly berries that had been carried into the house, he hovered round its windows and doors with anxious and curious stealth. Just then the window was opened, and along its outside ledge something was strewn by a careful hand. From a standard rose-bush, whither he had flown when the window was opened, our little friend watched the affair. Was there any risk to be feared? All seemed quiet and still. Should he venture? In another minute he was on the ledge, and boldly devouring crumb after crumb of the scattered bread. A burst of delighted laughter from within sent him back with sudden flight to the rose-bush. But no disaster ensued, and he was tempted again and again. The children within might well laugh at the saucy bird whom their father had, by his gift of bread-crumbs, tempted to the place, but it was a laugh that told of nothing but kind delight.

' "Little bits of things do accidentally turn up always, indeed!" said the little robin to himself, as he crept into his ivy hole that evening to sleep; and he dreamt half the night of the wonderful place and the princely fare. And next morning, perched in the laurel bush near the tortoise's retreat, he told his sleeping friend the long, marvellous tale of his yesterday's adventures, and promised him more news against the time when he should return to wake him up in the spring. There was no doubt that robin had soon plenty to tell. He had to tell not only of the meal that was spread for him in due time that very Christmas day by those suddenly raised up friends – but of the daily meal that henceforth never failed; of the friendly faces that sat around the breakfast-table on which at last he was allowed to hop about at will; of how he used to sing on the rose-tree outside, every morning of every day, to welcome the waking of his friends, and how, in the late afternoons, the father would sometimes open the window, and sit there alone by himself, listening to his song.

' "Come, come, my little friend," remarked the tortoise, when he did awake at last. "I have been asleep for a long time, and I dare say have been dreaming all manner of fine things myself, if I could but think of them. Now, I suspect you have had a nap as well. However, I am very glad to see you alive, and not so half-starved looking as I expected. But as to your having sung every day, and had plenty to eat every day, and been so happy all the time, – take my advice, don't try to cram older heads than your own with traveller's tales!"'

Mrs Margaret Gatty (1807–73)
from *Parables from Nature*

Several other books on the robin were published, mostly anonymously, during the nineteenth century[81]. There were also many short books for children, some with garish illustrations and worse poems under the title *Robin Redbreast* or similar. These continued into the twentieth century. Ernest Nister even published his *Robin Redbreast* in the shape of a robin in silhouette. A more substantial contribution was Lady Lindsay's *About Robins* (1889), a collection of poems and stories from previous writers, with some original matter.

After about 1850, people allowed themselves to write solely for the enjoyment of children. Robins still found their way into stories for young children but became rare in stories for older children. None could find their way on to Treasure Islands, or to Wonderland or even into Lear's poems. A robin makes an appearance in a racy tale by George Manville Fenn (1831-1909), *The Story of Mrs Puss, Boxer, Specklems the Starling, and the Robin*. Fenn was a popular thriller writer and in this story, the robin, typically, is the friend

---

[81] Examples are *Burford Cottage and its Robin Redbreast*, 1835, by 'The Author of Keeper's Travels', where a robin listens for 476 pages to conversations; *The Robins of Woodside Lodge*, 1850, by 'Aunt E.', a narrative-poem about a tame robin which fell into a milkpail and nested in a beehive; *The Robin's Nest and Where do you think they built it?*, 1863, by 'A Clergyman's Wife', about life round a village church in which the robins nested; *The Personal Experiences of Robin the Bold*, 1873, by 'the Author of *Life Underground*', an interwoven tale of robins and humans; *The One-legged Robin*, 1879, by a 'Manchester Pythagorean' about a tame robin and robin-lore; and *The Robin's Christmas Eve*, c. 1880, by 'C.E.B.' a verse about a robin in a church at Christmas. There are others.

of the dog and persuades other birds to help him remove a thorn from his nose.

One particularly fine exception is Frances Hodgson Burnett's *The Secret Garden*. The robin, though still anthropomorphic to an extent, is much more like a genuine robin. The story begins with a description of Mary Lennox as 'the most disagreeable-looking child ever seen', unwanted by her parents, being brought up in India by an 'ayah' (nurse). When her parents and the ayah die of a cholera epidemic she is sent to a misanthropic uncle who lives in a grand manor house in Yorkshire. She starts to explore the grounds and hears about a garden that has been locked up for ten years:

> 'She could see the tops of trees above the wall, and when she stood still she saw a bird with a bright red breast sitting on the topmost branch of one of them, and suddenly he burst into his winter song – almost as if he had caught sight of her and was calling to her.

> 'She stopped and listened to him, and somehow his cheerful, friendly little whistle gave her a pleased feeling – even a disagreeable little girl may be lonely … and the bright-breasted little bird brought a look into her sour little face which was almost a smile. She listened to him until he flew away. He was not like an Indian bird, and she liked him and wondered if she should ever see him again. Perhaps he lived in the mysterious garden and knew all about it.

> [She explains what she has seen to the gardener.]

> 'To her surprise the surly old weather-beaten face actually changed its expression. A slow smile spread over it and the gardener looked quite different. It made her think that it was curious how much nicer a person looked when he smiled. She had not thought of it before.

> 'He turned about to the orchard side of his garden and

began to whistle – a low, soft whistle. She could not understand how such a surly man could make such a coaxing sound.

'Almost the next moment a wonderful thing happened. She heard a soft little rushing flight through the air – and it was the bird with the red breast flying to them, and he actually alighted on the big clod of earth quite near to the gardener's foot.

'"Here he is," chuckled the old man, and then he spoke to the bird as if he were speaking to a child.

'"Where has tha' been tha' cheeky little beggar?" he said "I've not seen thee before today. Has tha' been courtin' this early in th' season? Tha'rt too for'ard."

'The bird put his tiny head on one side and looked up at him with his soft bright eye, which was like a black dewdrop. He seemed quite familiar and not the least afraid. He hopped about and pecked the earth briskly, looking for seeds and insects. It actually gave Mary a queer feeling in her heart, because he was so pretty and cheerful and seemed so like a person. He had a tiny plump body and a delicate beak, and slender delicate legs.

[The robin later shows her the key of the garden. Next visit to the garden she is skipping and the robin finds her.] 'He had followed her and he greeted her with a chirp. As Mary had skipped towards him she felt something heavy in her pocket strike against her at each jump, and when she saw the robin she laughed again.

' "You showed me where the key was yesterday," she said. "You ought to show me the door today; but I don't believe you know!"

'The robin flew from his swinging spray of ivy on to the top of the wall and he opened his beak and sang a loud, lovely trill, merely to show off. Nothing in the world is quite as adorably lovely as a robin when he shows off – and they are nearly always doing it.

'Mary Lennox had heard a great deal about Magic in her Ayah's stories, and she always said what happened almost at that moment was Magic.... Mary had stepped close to the robin, and suddenly the gust of wind swung aside some loose ivy trails, and more suddenly still she jumped towards it and caught it in her hand. This she did because she had seen something under it – a round knob which had been covered by the leaves hanging over it. It was the knob of a door.'

Frances Hodgson Burnett (1849-1924),
from *The Secret Garden* (1911)

This great mass of stories and poems about the robin for British children has no counterpart in other European countries. There are some translations of English tales, but otherwise, I only know of one short Breton Story, *Jean Rouge-Gorge*, in *Le Foyer Breton* by Emile Souvestre (1806-1854), and a sentimental anonymous German tale, in *The Redbreast and other Tales from the German* (1843) concerned, significantly, with a captive robin.

In the twentieth century, natural history books that included accurate descriptions and photographs of the real lives of animals began to replace imaginative anthropomorphic tales. An early example is *The Adventures of Cock Robin and his Mate*, by the pioneering bird photographer, Richard Kearton (1904). There have been plenty of others and more are continually being produced. In 1953, the *Robin* became the title of a weekly magazine. This was a companion magazine to the *Eagle*, the *Swift*, and *Girl*, explicitly intended for the youngest readers with strip cartoons featuring the likes of Andy Pandy, Woppit and Snip and Snap. It was a natural successor to children's chap-books. It folded in 1969 with the wide availability of television.

Who Killed Cock Robin? has become a well-known nursery rhyme and some others were quoted with it in Chapter 2. The song that includes 'The red, red robin goes bob-, bob-, bobbin' along' is actually about an American robin, though frequently illustrated with a European one. Here are a few more nursery rhymes[82]:

> The north wind doth blow,
> And we shall have snow,
> And what will poor robin do then?
> > Poor thing.
> He'll sit in a barn,
> And keep himself warm,
> And hide his head under his wing,
> > Poor thing.

> Pit, pat, well-a-day,
> Little Robin flew away;
> Where can little Robin be?
> Gone into the cherry tree.

> Little Bob Robin,
> Where do you live?
> Up in yonder hazel wood, sir,
> On a hazel twig.

> Little Robin Redbreast sat upon a tree,
> Up went pussy cat and down went he;
> Down came pussy, and away Robin ran;
> Says little Robin Redbreast, Catch me if you can.
> Little Robin Redbreast jumped upon a wall,
> Pussy cat jumped after him, and almost got a fall;
> Little Robin chirped and sang, and what did pussy say?
> Pussy cat said 'mew', and Robin jumped away.

---

[82] For these and others, see *Sing-Song: A Nursery Rhyme Book* (1872) and Iona and Peter Opie (1955) *The Oxford Nursery Rhyme Book*.

Little Robin Redbreast
Came to visit me;
This is what he whistled,
'Thank you for my tea.'

Bread and milk for breakfast,
  And woollen frocks to wear,
And a crumb for robin redbreast
  On the cold days of the year.

Wrens and robins in the hedge,
Wrens and robins here and there
Building, perching, pecking, fluttering,
Everywhere!

Several of the poems quoted elsewhere in this book have been
included in anthologies for children. These further poems were
written expressly for children:

The Blossom

Merry merry sparrow
  Under leaves so green
A happy blossom
  Sees you swift as arrow
Seek your cradle narrow
  Near my bosom.

Pretty, pretty robin!
  Under leaves so green,
A happy blossom
  Hears you sobbing, sobbing,
Pretty, pretty robin,
  Near my bosom.

William Blake (1757–1827), from *Songs of Innocence*

Robin Redbreast
(A Child's Song)

Good-bye, good-bye to summer!
  For summer's nearly done;
The garden smiling faintly,
  Cool breezes in the sun;
Our thrushes now are silent,
  Our swallows flown away, -
But Robin's here, in coat of brown,
  With ruddy breast-knot gay.
Robin, Robin Redbreast,
  O Robin dear!
Robin singing sweetly
  In the falling of the year.

Bright yellow, red, and orange,
  The leaves come down in hosts;
The trees are Indian Princes,
  But soon they'll turn to Ghosts;
The scanty pears and apples
  Hang russet on the bough,
It's autumn, autumn, autumn late,
  'Twill soon be winter now.
Robin, Robin Redbreast,
  O Robin dear!
And welaway! My Robin,
  For pinching times are near.

The fireside for the cricket,
  The wheatstack for the mouse,
When trembling night-winds whistle
  And moan all round the house;
The frosty ways like iron,
  The branches plumed with snow, -
Alas! in winter, dead and dark,
  Where can poor Robin go?

Robin, Robin Redbreast,
  O Robin dear!
And a crumb of bread for Robin,
  His little heart to cheer.

William Allingham (1824–89)

Summer fading, winter comes –
Frosty mornings, tingling thumbs,
Window robins, winter rooks,
And the picture story books.

Robert Louis Stevenson (1850-1894),
in A Child's Garden of Verses

The Robin[83]

The Robin is the fairies' page;
  They keep him neatly dressed
For country service or for town
In dapper livery of brown
  And little scarlet vest.

On busy errands all day long
  He hurries to and fro
With watchful eyes and nimble wings –
There are not very many things
  The robin doesn't know.

And he can tell you, if he will,
  The latest fairy news:
The quaint adventures of the King,

---

[83] Rose Fyleman's work was mostly about fairies. It seems she has deliberately mixed robin redbreast with Robin Goodfellow in this poem.

And whom the Queen is visiting,
And where she gets her shoes.

And lately when the fairy Court
Invited me to tea,
He stood behind the Royal Chair;
And here I solemnly declare,
When he discovered I was there,
That Robin *winked* at me.

Rose Fyleman (1877–1957),
from *The Fairy Green* (1919)

Sir Robin's Wooing[84]

Sir Robin came a-courting with a Bold Brave Air,
He gazed at all the garden with a Bright Little Stare.
He ruffled up a feather
And put his wing together,
Oh, Robin came a-courting with a Bold Brave Air

His little lady watched him from a Near By Tree,
Said he, 'I am the finest fellow You'll Ever See.'
He pertled up and down,
In the suit of red and brown,
And danced a little polka with a One, Two, Three!

She turned her little back on him and Said Not a Word,
And made Sir Robin feel he was a <u>Very</u> Small Bird.
Thought he, 'What shall I do?
How can a Robin woo
A lady whose behaviour is so Very Ab-Surd.'

---

[84] In the original there were new lines for each capitalised word (except Robin). Note the reference to courtship feeding.

He sidled up and said to her, 'Dear Wee Thing,
Let me fetch a worm for you and Hear Me Sing,
Your eyes are black and bright,
You're just the sweetest mite,
Oh, isn't there a single thing you'd like Me to Bring!'

And then she nestled up to him as He Sat There,
She asked him if he <u>really</u> thought They'd Make A good Pair.
She was easy to convince,
For I haven't seen them since
Sir Robin came a-courting with a Brave Bold Air.

Enid Blyton (1897–1968)

Chapter 12
A Happy Christmas

When we think of Christmas, we think of robins. Every year at Christmas time, not only will the garden robin come for scraps from the bird table or feeder, but somewhere around the house there will almost certainly be Christmas cards depicting robins.

No doubt it is this association with winter and its reputation as the domestic bird that has tied it in with Christmas. But there is another connection: with the very notion of postage and so, specifically, with Christmas cards. There are many more robins on Christmas cards than any other bird. They are also an integral part of Christmas wishes, sometimes appearing on cards with otherwise religious themes. They have appeared on Christmas stamps, and in 1959 and again in 2001, all five of the British Christmas stamps depicted robins (see front endpaper). The origin of this link is demonstrated by Jemima, the cook at Framley Parsonage, who addressed a real postman:

'Come in, robin postman, and warm theeself awhile.'

Anthony Trollope,
from *Framley Parsonage* (1861)

We are so used to the navy blue worn by postmen, it seems odd that they should be nicknamed 'robins', as have some groups with red uniforms (Chapter 8). But Trollope worked in the Post Office in 1860 and, at that time, the postman also wore a red coat. Red was the royal colour for the Royal Mail. It was not universally admired. Punch, for instance, headed a protest 'The Post Office in a Blaze', after it was found that the military style of the uniforms 'alarmed half of the old ladies in London'. The red colour also showed the dirt. It was changed in 1861 to dark blue, with red facings. The nickname presumably vanished soon afterwards, but not before Christmas cards had become popular. The colour red remains on letter boxes, Royal Mail vans - and on robins on Christmas cards.

To look through the stationery of the Victorian period is to look at social history. When Christmas cards and Christmas letter-paper first became popular, around 1860, a robin was the standard symbol. However, it was not only at Christmas that robins were seen on cards.

Valentine cards, which were popular before Christmas cards, also had them. Valentines tended to be much more elaborate than early Christmas cards. One of about 1850 has a robin carrying a letter alongside some flowers and, above the bird: 'The little general postman'. The Valentine shown opposite (its envelope postmarked 14 February 1861) stated 'I love you' and, above the robin, 'A message by the morning Post'. A few Valentines of the later nineteenth century had robins on them, although by then robins had largely disappeared from Valentines. The few remaining were probably old Christmas card stocks.

Christmas cards were preceded by Christmas notepaper. The earliest dated example that I know of bears a watermark of 1859. This was probably one of the first years in which such paper became common, making it a late addition to the early Victorian fashion for ornamental stationery that included valentines, steel-engraved letter-headings, cards celebrating a variety of occasions, calling cards, or cards for general use. Christmas cards rapidly became the most popular of all and outlived most of the rest, although cards for numerous minor celebrations have reappeared in the last few decades. The early letter paper often had a large engraving of a view or of some figures, while below there might be a message, or verses. At Christmas, this was replaced with a coloured picture of robins and holly.

A rather different, but probably contemporary, type of paper was more restrained. This was similar to private letter paper with an embossed crest. At Christmas, it was headed by a small, stylized robin, heavily embossed, set in or above a scroll saying 'A merry Christmas'. Similar notepaper for the New Year had a bunch of flowers with 'A happy New Year', but the two were combined a little later. The embossed design often appeared on the envelope, too. This set was part of a traveller's sample that must date from 1862 as it includes the linked British and Danish flags. It celebrates the arrival of Princess Alexandra of Denmark, whose marriage with Edward Prince of Wales took place in March 1863.

Christmas notepaper was quickly replaced by Christmas cards. Early Christmas cards were mostly small and oblong with a formal, stylised robin and scroll similar to that on the notepaper. The edge was scalloped or outlined in colour (see back endpaper), and the envelope matched. Modelled on the calling-card, this card had a robin and scroll in place of the name. By the mid-1870s, cards had become more elaborate. The robin is sometimes shown with a letter in its beak and even lifting the knocker of a door. One shows a robin with two dangling threads from its beak each with a tiny letter that can be opened to read 'A merry Christmas'; and 'A happy New Year'. The card is headed 'A little gentleman much sought after at Christmas time, the postman'.

At first, all the cards were made in England, but after a few years, cheap colour reproduction was perfected in Germany. This then dominated the European market. Many colour pictures were sold for scrap-albums, and Christmas cards then often had a colour picture pasted in the centre. The robins were usually depicted in natural poses, and the cards became larger and more elaborate. By the late 1870s, the original stylized calling-card type disappeared. By then, too, some of the cards were made as folded sheets (like the valentines), while others were set in a framework of intricate lace-like paper (see back endpaper). The robin ceases to be a plain portrait and is shown perched among holly or in a little winter scene. Some of the pictures could be lifted to reveal a Christmas message.

One card even shows a robin perched on a trap, surely most inappropriate at Christmas! Similar illustrations appeared in bird books and presumably this one was copied, its German printers totally misconstruing the British interest in robins.

By the 1890s, Christmas cards had become extraordinarily elaborate. Some included pop-up figures or little paper levers to separate the various parts of the picture. A particularly complicated example shows a cock robin feeding its hen in a nesting-box. By pulling a lever, the box becomes three-dimensional, with the cock robin on a perch outside. Another example has robins feeding in the snow outside the doors of a house, and these doors can be opened to show a ballroom with dancers. Another one shows a single robin feeding in the snow, with the inscription: 'Behind Master Robin but let the light fall, in swarms his companions will come to his call'. When the card is held to the light, many other robins, painted on the back, are seen coming down. Some cards had stitched pictures in silk on a scented sachet, or had cotton wool for snow, real moss for vegetation, and even real feathers for the robin (eliciting protests).

In the twentieth century, Christmas cards reverted to a simpler form. Robins are shown in every natural, and many unnatural, attitudes. They are sometimes depicted in small groups or flocks. In nature, such individuals would fight immediately, so this is another inappropriate statement for Christmas.

Robins only occur with any frequency on British cards. Some countries do have substitutes, for example, in Finland some cards depict bullfinches, which come around the houses at this season of the year.

One final link with Christmas derives from the habit of feeding robins in winter. In the late nineteenth century, the name was used for 'a little boy or girl beggar standing about like a starving robin' and the 'Robin dinner' appeared:

> 'due to the kindly suggestion of the Rev. Charles Bullock, editor of *Home Words*, who appeals to the generosity of his readers to enable him to entertain 25,000 or 30,000 London children every year.'

> J. Redding Ware, in *Passing English of the Victorian Era* (1909)

Elaborate Christmas card of 1890

1850s Valentine card

J M W Turner (1775-1851) painted a series of birds in watercolour during visits to Farnley Hall, in Yorkshire, between 1816 and 1819. Most were from dead specimens but this robin was from life. In all, the concentration on colour and detail demonstrates his fascination with birds

Christmas card of a robin on a trap from a German printer of the late 19th century

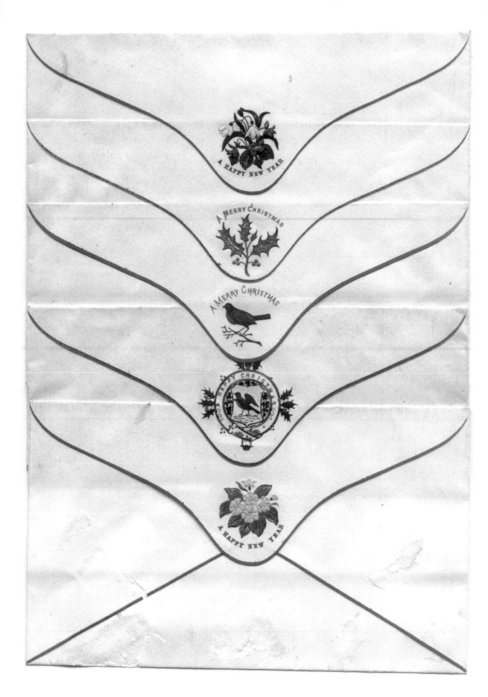

Victorian Christmas card envelopes, with embossed backs

My wishes come by Robin's rhymes,
Since he has pleased so many times;
For London poor are still in need,
Whom robin's crumbs may help to feed.

Or, if the Missions we would aid
By Christmas cards and sheets, now made,
The Robin gladly will take flight,
With wings of love he'll bear your mite.

Each Christmas offering to our King,
Each feeble prayer may blessings bring;
May blessings rest on you, my friend,
True Christmas joys that never end.

Anonymous (c. 1860), quoted from a paper among the
Christmas cards in the Victoria and Albert Museum, London

Christmas cards have long contained rhymes, mostly sentimental, but occasionally they go further:

To a Robin who Roosted in a Holly Bough set by a Christmas Crib

What were you thinking of, Robin o' Red,
Coming to Church to rest your head?
Was it once on a strange-wrought day
You went to a Tree on a hill far away
To take one pain from a thorn-pierced Head,
And bore the blood to your breast instead?

What are you dreaming of, Robin o' Red,
Fast asleep in your holly tree bed?
Is it that love, red love, brings pain
Ere wrong can be turned to right again?
That Christmas holly's as sharp as thorn

Every time that the Christ is born?
That after the Crib comes the Cross; the Tomb
Emptied, that He might lift our doom?
That right to the end of the hangman's rope,
Through all the follies of man there's hope?

So cheer us, Robin, each Christmastide,
With thoughts of the One who came, who died,
Who rose again, and made all new;
Who gave Himself to make us true –
Thank you, Robin o' Red, thank you.

Canon S. Prideaux (1949)

Said the robin to the sparrow
'I should really like to know
Why these anxious human beings
Rush about and worry so.'

Said the Sparrow to the robin
'Friend, I think that it must be
That they have no Heavenly Father
Such as cares for you and me.'

Elizabeth Cheyney (early 20th century?)

The inclusion of the robin in otherwise religious Christmas imagery has been taken up by some others.

A Turn for the Better

'Now I Joseph was walking and I walked not...'
(Book of James or Protevangelium)

Now I Joseph was walking, and I walked not,
Between the allotments on a December morning.
The clouds were mauve as a crocus, peeling back petals,
And a sparse pollen of snow came parping down
On the bare ground and greenhouse groins and dun
Tight-head chrysanthemums crumpled by the frost.
The cock in the hen-run blustered to its perch
On the lid of the swill-bucket, rattled its red
At the fluttering flakes, levered its throat open –
And not a croak creaked out.
        I looked about me:
 The snow was stock-still in the sky like pluckings
Of cotton wool glued on a grocer's window,
And down in the brown of the dyke, a smoky feather
Let on a robin's head, between the black
Glass-ally eyes and the gimlet beak,
And never a flick it gave to shake it off.
Workmen on the electric cable track
Swing picks in the air and held them there, rigid
Raised bait to mouths and never took a bite.
One putting up a hand to scratch his head,
Shifted the peak of his cap a couple of inch,
And never scratched. A dead leaf drifting
Hung bracketed against the wire netting
Like a pin caught on a magnet.
        For at that minute,
Making was made, history rolled
Backward and forward in time, memory was unfolded
Like a quick discovery, old habits were reinvented,
Old phrases coined. The tree grew down
Into its sapling self, the sapling into the seed.

Cobbles of wall and slate of rafters
Were cleft and stratified again as rock,
And the rock unweathered itself a cloud-height higher,
And the sea flowed over it. A brand-new now
Stretched on either hand to then and someday,
Might-have and perhaps.
          Then suddenly the cock
Coughed up its crow, the robin skittered off
And the snow fell like a million pound of shillings,
And out of the beginning always of the world
I heard the cry of a child.

Norman Nicholson (1914-1987),
from *The Pot Geranium* (1954)

Aunt Mary's Tree

Now of all the trees by the king's highway,
Which do I love the best?
O! the one that is green upon Christmas Day,
The bush with the bleeding breast.
Now the holly with her drops of blood for me:
For that is our dear Aunt Mary's tree.

Its leaves are sweet with our Saviour's Name,
'Tis a plant that loves the poor:
Summer and winter it shines the same,
Besides the cottage door.
O! the holly with her drops of blood for me:
For that is our kind Aunt Mary's tree.

'Tis a bush that the birds will never leave:
They sing in it all day long;
But sweetest of all upon Christmas Eve,
Is to hear the robin's song.

'Tis the merriest sound upon earth and sea:
For it comes from our own Aunt Mary's tree.

So of all that grow by the king's highway,
I love that tree the best:
'Tis a bower for the birds upon Christmas Day,
The bush of the bleeding breast.
O! the holly with her drops of blood for me:
For that is our sweet Aunt Mary's tree.

R.S. Hawker (1803–1875), from Cornish Ballads

Carol

What is Christmas without
snow? We need it
as bread of a cold
climate, ermine to trim

our sins with, a brief
sleeve for charity's
scarecrow to wear its heart
on, bold as a robin.

R.S. Thomas (1913–2000)

from *Carol of the Birds*

Robins and hidden wrens whose shiny notes
Tinsel the precincts of the winter sun.

Anne Stevenson (b. 1933)

For others, the Christmas connection is quite different:

The Christmas Robin

The snows of February had buried Christmas
Deep in the woods, where grew self-seeded
The fir-trees of a Christmas yet unknown,
Without a candle or a strand of tinsel.

Nevertheless when, hand in hand, plodding
Between the frozen ruts, we lovers paused
And 'Christmas trees!' cried suddenly together,
Christmas was there again, as in December.

We velveted our love with fantasy
Down a long vista row of Christmas trees,
Whose coloured candles slowly guttered down
As grandchildren came trooping round our knees.

But he knew better, did the Christmas robin –
The murderous robin with his breast aglow
And legs apart, in a spade-handle perched:
He prophesied more snow, and worse than snow.

Robert Graves (1895-1985),
from *Collected Poems* (1938)

Real Life Christmas Card

Robin, I watch you. You are a perfect robin –
except, shouldn't you be perched on a spade handle?

Robin, you watch me. Am I a perfect man – except,
shouldn't I have a trap in my pocket, a gun in my hand?

I, too, am in my winter plumage, not unlike yours,
except, the red is in my breast, not on it.

You sing your robin song, I my man song. They're different,
but they mean the same: winter, territory, greed.

Will we survive, bold eyes, to pick
the seeds in the ground, the seeds in my mind?

The snow man thinks so. Look at his silly smile
slushily spilling down the scarf I gave him.

Norman MacCaig (1910-1996)

After Christmas

On New Year's Eve one robin tracked our stride
A good two hundred yards along a hedge
(Or hedge and copse combined, the English way)
Until the path bent through the trees. We lay
Our lunchtime crumbs as end-of-year reward.
Today in woods in Kentish countryside
We saw them, in their scores, ignite inside
Each thicket's heart a ticking pulse of red –
As if there'd been a mantelpiece migration.
We were surprised, almost, on our return,
To find that every silent branch or ledge,
On every card, was still safe-occupied.

Peter Walton, from *The Cheerfulness of Sparrows* (1998)

The robin makes a passing appearance in many other Christmas poems.

Like us, robins have not always behaved well at Christmas. One tame robin was accustomed to hop on the table during meals:

> 'On a certain Christmas day he had his share of the plum pudding and brandy sauce, then retired to the back of a chair, and presently fell on the floor – drunk. He was lifted to a safe place where he could sleep off the effects. But once was enough, never again did he touch Christmas pudding.'

Margaret Holden, in Near Neighbours (1935)

I will let W.H. Davies, one of the twentieth century's greatest nature poets, close the book:

Peace and Goodwill

On Christmas day I sit and think,
Thoughts white as snow, and black as ink.
My nearest kinsman, turned a knave,
Robbed me of all that I could save.
When he was gone, and I was poor,
His sister yelped me from her door.

The Robin sings his Christmas song,
And no bird has a sweeter tongue.
God bless them all – my wife so true,
And pretty Robin Redbreast too.
God bless my kinsman far away,
And give his sister joy this day.

W.H. Davies (1871-1940),
from The Poet's Calendar (1927)

Index of authors

General index

Richard Mabey, who wrote the Foreword, is well-known for his consistent concern for world nature conservation. He edited *The Oxford Book of Nature* (1995) and *Flora Britannica* (1996). His many acclaimed books include *Gilbert White* (Whitbread Biography Award, 1986), *Whistling in the Dark: In Pursuit of Nightingales* (1994); Signed, limited edition (2007), *Nature Cure* (2005) and, with Mark Cocker, he co-edited the sister volume to *Flora Britannica* – *Birds Britannica* (2006).

Richard wrote the Preface for Stewart Beer's *An Exaltation of Skylarks* (SMH Books,1995), which was to become a triple-award-winner.

Euan Dunn, MBE, was on the staff of the Edward Grey Institute (1970-1976; under David Lack until 1973). At the EGI, he was routinely called-upon to draw the poster campaign cartoon which advertised the annual student conference. He drew acclaimed cartoons for Denis Summers-Smith's *In Search of Sparrows*. Currently head of Marine Policy at the RSPB, he revels in a genre that allows him to combine his love of birds, illustration, and a 'subversive' (his words) sense of humour.

'**Terence Lambert** must stand as one of the finest and most imaginative bird painters alive today. His illustrative technique alone is remarkable, his fastidious eye for the details of plumage and perch. Yet it is his ability to enter a bird's universe, his intuitive sense of the intensity and priorities of its life that sets him apart.'

(THE TIMES)